To:
Sus

bless others
God keep you au..
Thank you for
your support!

Jessica C. Williams

HEALING
PAST ✦
WOUNDS

HEALING
PAST
WOUNDS

Redefining Your Now By Living Free
From Trauma, Shame, and Unforgiveness

JESSICA C. WILLIAMS

**WARRIOR
WOMEN IN
*Christ***

Warrior Women in Christ, LLC

Healing Past Wounds: Redefining Your Now By Living Free From Trauma, Shame, and Unforgiveness

First published in Goose Creek, South Carolina, by Warrior Women In Christ, LLC

Edited by My Sweet Midwife, Harriet "D.C." T.

First edition 2023

For more information on the publisher, email info@warriorwomenic.com

ISBN: 979-8-9880188-0-3 (Paperback)
ISBN: 979-8-9880188-1-0 (E-Book)

Dedicated to the one true God. He alone has healed me from many wounds.

To you, God's chosen warriors:

May your past wounds be healed. May every tear you've cried and the pain you've endured not be in vain. May you walk in freedom and truth.

Contents

Foreword

In the trauma arena, where hope acts as a promise-breaker and trust is a constant liar, Jessica Williams chooses to step into the ring and heal. "Healing Past Wounds: Redefining Your Now by Living Free from Trauma, Shame and Unforgiveness" links arms with the wounded souls, the broken spirits, the unworthy hearts, and the voiceless victims. With great courage and an even greater commitment to fully embrace God's truth, Jessica reveals every element of her trauma. She holds nothing back because healing means freedom. Her voice resounds with anguish and disbelief, as would anyone who has kept silent in the areas of family rejection, sexual abuse, incest, and even abortion. And though these areas only scratch the surface of her past traumas, Jessica shows us in "Healing Past Wounds," healing is possible.

I believe friendships forge out of the unlikeliest situations, as do Godly intersections. Simply put, a pandemic brought Jessica to my social media doorstep. As our circles intersected, so did parts of our narrative. I watched how this Warrior Women in Christ founder put into service her spiritual resources into prayer and teaching while God encouraged me to share my tough and tenderness with women through Instagram. Through acts of intersected obedience, stories are shared, and in return, avenues for deeper intimacy with God are open for travel. This book becomes a conduit for women to acknowledge their woundedness and soon walk into the understanding of their true identity.

- You no longer walk as a wounded soul in Christ but as a new creation.

- In Christ, you no longer display the shards of a broken spirit but a blessed and holy vessel.

- In Christ, you no longer beat an unworthy heart but a steady rhythm resounding with gratitude and praise.

- In Christ, you no longer resign as a voiceless victim but as a voice that cannot stay silent anymore!

Jessica packs overwhelming and diverse content into this vulnerable offering. But it is her beautiful vulnerability that beckons her to this traumatic arena. Throughout these pages, you'll find her real and raw stories of hope and experience of how God's healing of past wounds can always be trusted. It's time to redefine your now by living free from your trauma, shame, and unforgiveness. I invite you to join Jessica throughout the pages of her book as God heals your past wounds.

Doris M. Cush

Writer + Encourager

IG: @dmcushite

Important Note From The Author

Move forward with caution

Some chapters contain sensitive content which can trigger traumatic memories for the reader. Although I'm pretty sure trauma, shame, unforgiveness, or past wounds brought you here. Nevertheless, if you know you may be triggered by any of the content but still want to proceed, I encourage you to read this book with a therapist, pastor, or a small group. If you are currently dealing with any form of abuse and need help now, please head to the end of this book and search the "Further Reading and Resources" section.

Every story in this book is true. Most names, locations, and undeniable details have been changed to protect the privacy of those that are not ready to deal with or acknowledge their portion in creating most of the wounds discussed throughout the chapters.

Please read before moving forward

As an ordained minister of the gospel, my views in this book have a bib-lical foundation and should be taken into consideration while moving forward. This book is broken down into two sections. The first half is presented in memoir style as I discuss and share some of my personal wounds. The second half is written to share the process I took in healing. Opening an opportunity to bring you, the reader, into the story and self-reflect. Sharing practical tips and steps for healing your past wounds.

My prayer is this book will help you begin your journey of healing. Not to answer every question but to help start your process. It's important to acknowledge that many of our wounds are deeply rooted in; Trauma, Rejection, and Unforgiveness (T.R.U.). But as you continue to go before Jesus with what's been T.R.U. in your life, allow Him to reveal His Truth and deeply heal your past wounds caused by others or self-inflicted. Nevertheless, today, I encourage you to ponder the following question: Are you doing right by you?

Listen; you have a serious choice to make. Will you choose the path of healing or the one where you stay wounded? They both hurt; trust me, I know both feelings too well. Yet, only one has freedom, growth, and wholeness. The other keeps you in bondage, fear, and stagnation, only offering temporary fixes. Those fixes cause more destruction to one's self. The decision is yours. Whichever you decide, you must live with the outcome.

God's Word is real, solid, and accurate. I put it into practice myself. I've witnessed the power of His Word in others, and honestly, it's essential for our well-being, especially as believers of Christ Jesus. Let's be honest; I'm not saying life will be easy once healed. What I am saying is you are not alone. God has given us tools to help us grow and become more robust. And as each wound is healed, He is restoring you to reach back and help another.

Let me remind you of God's Word: "Many are called, but few are chosen" (Matthew 22:14). Let me put some numbers to this, 70% of adults in the U.S. have experienced some type of traumatic event at least once in their lives. That's a total of 223.4 million people.[1] Many of the 70% may never heal. But God has called you and actually chose you to heal by taking the steps to embrace a new life narrative. It doesn't matter what you have done or what has been done to you. God is calling His daughters in this hour. He can use your brokenness and turn it into beauty. He can restore what you thought was lost and improve it. The power of repentance, forgiveness, and faith are great weapons during this journey. Will you accept God's invitation of Grace and healing?

Love,

Jess

"Until you heal the wounds of your past, you are going to bleed.

You can bandage the bleeding with food, with alcohol, with sex;

but eventually, it will all ooze through and stain your life.

You must find the strength to open the wounds, stick your hands inside,

pull out the core of the pain that is

holding you in your past, the memories, and make peace with them."

- Iyanla Vanzant

Part I

ACKNOWLEDGING THE WOUNDS

"A wound that goes unacknowledged and unwept is a wound that cannot heal." - John Eldredge

To My Wounded Sister

Our wounds are often the openings into the best and most beautiful part of us. - David Richo

WE OFTEN WALK AROUND hurt, unhealed, and broken from our past. We tend to cover up those deep wounds with small band-aids. Yet, in reality, each wound becomes more infected, creating a bigger problem, essentially killing us internally and externally. We move about in life as if those wounds will heal under the bandages, never genuinely looking to analyze the depth of each one. As wounded people, we tend to create lies about ourselves and others, masking the real pain within us.

Like many of you reading this book, I have experienced deep wounds from my past. However, the deepest scares came from trauma, rejection, and unforgiveness. Self-trust, pride, and my lack of faith in God became constant obstacles. On the quest towards healing, I had to be honest; my healing wasn't going to come without change. Internally, I blamed others for my actions, positioning myself as a constant victim instead of owning my portion and changing what I could control. Externally, I put up a good front. I laughed often, kept conversations surface-level, suppressed my feelings, and hid my past and true beliefs so others could not get close enough to judge me. Deeper relationships required a vulnerability I was not willing to offer.

When looking further into the word "wound," it's simply defined as an injury to living tissue caused by a cut, blow, or another impact, typically in which the skin is cut or broken. To inflict an injury on (someone) .[2]Why do we walk around with old wounds? It's far easier to ignore a problem by covering it with temporary fixes than to have the damage evaluated and taken care of properly. Most of us can be afraid to face the root cause of our wounds, and feeling this way can only lead to other injuries because we choose to keep our past a secret. Deep wounds hurt a lot more than those minor surface ones. And not many of us want to feel pain again, even to help heal and free us from those past cuts, blows, and impacts.

I challenge you to think about the following:

- What are some of the wounds you walk around with?

- Do you know where they originated?

We often tend not to seek God until we have looked to ourselves and others for the answers. Most of us have turned to alcohol or drugs to suppress abuse, leading to anxiety or depression. We experience the loss of a loved one and lose ourselves, or worse yet, we have thoughts of wanting to take our own lives. We experience relational hurt and seek to hurt others, so we aren't the only ones walking around with that pain. The cycle can feel endless, causing pain as we live wounded and unhealed. We tend to put more faith in our GPS systems' every turn instead of depending on the one and only true God to direct our paths fully. Because of our selfish nature, we tend to block our healing because we are not truly ready. A small portion of us have made being unhealed such a massive part of our personal story, and we engrave it into our DNA.

Along my healing journey, God met me where I was at every turn, just like He will meet you. I needed to know God was real, so I sought Him. When I did, I started healing through His word. Although this didn't happen overnight, vulnerability overtook me as I confessed my sins and acknowledged my wounds caused by others. I grew a heart of repentance, which led to healing, increased faith, and my true identity in Christ Jesus. Building a personal relationship with God the Father, Son, and

Holy Spirit has freed me. His word is true when it says: "He heals the brokenhearted and binds up their wounds."[3] His word further informs us: "For I will restore health to you, and your wounds I will heal, declares the Lord, because they have called you an outcast: 'It is Zion, for whom no one cares!'"[4] Because of God's grace and mercy, I can look in the mirror and see my true reflection. I asked a straightforward question:

"Lord, please show me what areas in my life from past to present need healing?" He began showing me. Some wounds were more challenging to accept than others, but He was there, loving me through each process. Then it hit me: my life is not my own. My pain has a purpose, and I intend to help others heal from their past wounds. Even if it means being vulnerable and addressing elephants in the room, my voice can no longer remain silent. Fear of rejection had to go from my heart because YOU, the one reading this book, need my true story to help start your healing journey!

Let's heal together.

Therefore, confess your sins to one another and pray for one another that you may be healed. The prayer of a righteous person has great power as it is working. - James 5:16

2

His Eye Is On The Sparrow

Are not two sparrows sold for a penny? And not one of them will fall to the ground apart from your Father. But even the hairs on your head are all numbered. Fear not, therefore; you are of more value than many sparrows. - Matthew 10:29-31

SWEAT DRIPPED PROFUSELY FROM her caramel-brown, wrinkled skin. I watched nervously as those brown eyes turned black. I could see her soul slipping away, as it was only a matter of time before she would take her last breath. "I love you, Grandma. His eye is on the sparrow," I whispered.

She gasped for air and muscled enough strength to respond, saying, "I love you too. I know He watches over me."

"Oh, Grandma. Leah loves you too."

Tears dripped even faster, and her eyes began staring blankly into the depth of my soul.

"Grandma, did you hear me? Leah said she loves you too. I want to hear you say it back!"

Pausing between every word, she whispered,

"I...Love...Leah...too."

My heart felt a piercing pain as I knew it would be the last time we spoke. I slowly turned around, walked over to my friend, and told him I was ready to leave. While walking down the narrow hallway of the nursing home, it felt like I had walked into an enormous blurry photo. My focus was as if I was alone, and reality was setting in. Though my friend wondered why I wanted to leave, my only piercing response to his inquiry was:

"Because she is not there! I don't want to see my grandmother die!"

―――――◆○◆―――――

Holding back tears, a sinking feeling formed in my chest, and millions of thoughts raced through my head. The moment of true heartache took over. I was losing the closest person to me. The one I could count on most would no longer dwell on this earth. Who would now help me in my darkest moments? How will she ever know if I will become the woman she diligently prayed for me to be? Who is going to love me now?

Wearing a brave face for my younger sister, my friend and I walked into the house and was greeted by the prettiest light brown eyes and smile. My sister, Leah, always shined so brightly. Though I kept the dialogue positive, I told her what Grandma said. With a gleam in her eye, Leah smiled as she said, "I love her so much. I can't wait to see her next time."

Next time

It only took a few rings to turn my world upside down.

"Jessica, you must head to the hospital immediately; they are rushing your grandmother over!"

Instantly, I turned red and pale in the face. Thump, thump, thump... The sound of my heart beating was all I heard. Panic set in, and I suddenly forgot how to breathe. As much as I tried to calm myself to prepare for whatever, everything went out the window with a breath.

Leah, we have to go to the hospital.

"What, why?"

It's Grandma; she was rushed in.

"O, it's probably going to be OK, maybe like the last time."

And it is there my memory recalls moments like a quick flashing scene from a bad film.

Emergency room sign.

Walking through metal detectors. Silent words from a lady talking to me.

An unknown person gave her my grandmother's name.

Someone coming to get us.

My family sitting in a room.

Breaking down.

My piercing screams were heard outside the hospital.

People staring at me.

Outside.

My older brother Chris arrived at the hospital.

At that moment, life shifted. Emptiness became very familiar. I found myself facing everything head-on. Her pronounced death stirred up my deep mother-like heart wound. In the most surreal sense, her death left something dead in me. Perfect, she was not, but MY sparrow she was. The course of my journey changed drastically. I felt no one understood my loss or pain, or so I thought.

3

Orphan Baby

*He came unto his own, and his own received him not. -
John 1:11*

REJECTED. LONELY. ANGRY. FEARFUL.

These words described the morning of my fifth-grade graduation. My mom had to help someone else out, which meant she couldn't attend. My brother Chris still had school, and my sister Leah went to daycare, so I called my dad.

Hey Dad, umm, my fifth-grade graduation is today. Can you please come? My mom said she can't make it; Chris has to go to school, and Leah does too.

"Jessica, what time does the graduation start? I can't make any promises because you are telling me last minute. I have to work."

Tears began filling my eyes, and a warm sensation came over my body as thoughts of anger and rejection filled my mind. Hiding my emotions, Okay, Daddy, can you just take off work or go in late? Pretty, please try to make it because I don't want to be alone. It starts at 8:30 am, and it's going to be in the auditorium.

"Hmm, okay, we'll see, honey, because I still need to get dressed and drive to the school."

Alright, bye, Daddy. Unsure he would show up, I pulled myself together after we both said goodbye and wiped the tears from my eyes. I brushed my hair into a bun, threw on my favorite white polo-shirt dress, and darted out the door.

Late as usual, My 10-year-old eyes quickly scanned the auditorium and didn't see a soul from my family. I didn't want others to see my pain and disappointment, so I hid it behind my smile, found my class, and sat with them. I thought to myself,

"Now, when they call your name, keep walking out the door and go home."

The last thing I wanted was for others to ask me, "Where are your parents?" Now standing in line waiting to walk across the stage, I felt my legs starting to shake; I was embarrassed; my attire wasn't as fancy as my peers. I wondered if others would laugh or notice I dressed myself.

"Jessica, Jessica," I snapped back into reality as my teacher called my name. With a huge smile, I walked across the stage. As I followed my plan to walk straight out the door, who did I hear screaming and clapping for me? Yep, you guessed it. My Daddy! He came to support me with less than an hour's notice. My little pride was saved, and all hope was restored. This was one of the best days of my life. I held on to that moment for years.

———— ◆◇◆ ————

Rejection is something I felt all my life. Rejected by family, so-called friends, and strangers, it happened so much I allowed the negativity to become what I thought about day and night. I became closed off because of it and hid it very well under my laughs. But deep down, I had both mommy and daddy issues.

At age four, my parents separated. Although I was young and had no clue about grown people's issues, I was only concerned with who wanted me. Many believe children may not feel the pain of divorce when they are young. Unfortunately for me, I have memories that go back to infancy.

I remember my mom taking my older brother with her for a while, and my father said I couldn't live with him at the time either. So, I became known as "Family Baby." I mostly lived with my mom's parents, which is why my grandmother became my favorite person. I stayed nights with other family members as well. Yes, that name was cute for the time, but as I grew older, I felt more like "Orphan Baby."

As time passed, I hated seeing my parents because it meant I wasn't going home with either of them. For me, this period felt like 100 years, but in all actuality, it was probably only one year, if that. All I know is I went from living in a big house with my own room and massive bed to sharing a room with my brother, which I secretly called in my head "the one my parents wanted."

Going from a two-parent home to a single-parent home had its own challenges. It was as if my life had hit a reset button. Entering a new school added to my already drama-filled life. I fought a lot and was rejected by my peers for having long hair and a light-skin complexion. This created an environment from hell for me. My youthful mind blamed it all on the divorce. Fighting and rejection became what I knew and expected. Oh, man, was my life toxic. But I would have glimpses of hope when my brother and I would stay weekends with Dad or go on family trips with Mom or other family members. As time passed, I was still able to spend time with my grandmother as she had now moved in with us. Our village had grown, and I eventually got into a routine.

During the end of my seventh-grade school year, my dad, big brother, and other family members went on a Disney World trip. Oh, did we have a blast? But on the way home, our father decided to stay in Florida for a while. I was confused by the reasoning, but I hung onto every word he said. This time the blow was too heavy for me to carry sober-minded. Dad never did move back to Michigan. Triggered again, I felt rejected, as if my brother and I were not enough for him. My little heart broke, and I needed my dad to return and fix stuff in Michigan. I wanted so badly for him to regain his role as my knight in shining armor, just like he did at my fifth-grade graduation. Not to mention to slay the pain caused by some relatives on his side of the family. They rejected me the most. They, too, were "Christians," yet those very ones caused me tons of trauma from incest, molestation, and emotional, mental, and spiritual damage. I became broken and voiceless because of them.

Not all but most of Mom's family would turn a blind eye to my abuse and toxic upbringing. They would comment on my weight unknowingly, scaring me about my body. So I became bulimic. The rejection cycle caused me to create a victim mindset. All my relationships became surface-level. I kept a tiny group of close friends but never felt good enough for others. I pointed out my negative quirks so others couldn't hurt me. I blamed my lack of healing on everyone around me. I wanted my parents to fix all my problems.

Tell me about a broken young girl, and I'll show you an old picture of me. I felt like a child left to fend for herself in a world swallowing her whole daily.

4

A Toxic Fairytale

There are wounds that never show on the body that are deeper and more hurtful than anything that bleeds. ——
Laurell K. Hamilton

MY JOURNEY BEGAN WHEN I was 15, dating my 17-year-old boyfriend, Dre. He was very different and my first real relationship. When we first met, I felt like he was not the one, but against my better judgment, I went forward with exchanging numbers and building a relationship with him. At first, he would do little things like take me out to the movies, dinner, and church. He would buy me flowers and write me love notes to tell me how beautiful I was. He even had his own house.

While at the gas station one day, Dre went inside while I waited in the car. Some guys pulled up to the pump next to us, and while Dre was walking back to the car, he noticed one of the guys looking at me. After pumping the gas, he returned to the car, and as we drove away, he calmly asked if I knew them. I responded;

No, why?

"I saw one of them looking at you. Did you give him your number?"

I paused and looked at him as if he was crazy.

"Why would you ask me something crazy like that?"

His mood changed in the blink of an eye as he slapped me across my face and told me never to call him crazy again! I was so confused, angry, and hurt by his horrific action. How can he (or anyone) profess love and then hit you in the same breath? Crying and demanding he take me home, Dre apologized profusely and began crying, saying how he was dealing with so much. The thought of losing me was overwhelming, and he couldn't handle another loss. He promised never to hit me again, and I promised not to tell anyone he did.

Well, Dre broke his promise. In fact, he broke it hundreds of times. Every time he broke it, I would buy more make-up and wear clothes that covered the scars. He eventually got tired of us not having a sexual relationship, so the pressure to lose my virginity increased from 0 to 100. But I had a secret that would make him look at me differently. Thinking he would stop beating me and be there for me like he used to, I told him. I shared about all the trauma I had experienced and how I now wanted to wait for marriage. I didn't want to be forced into something I disagreed with. Although I attended church, part of me wanted to do right while the other existed. Dre held me after I told him my deep secret, but his eyes turned dark, and he gave me an ultimatum shortly after. Either I would willingly have sex with him, or he would take it. Hurt, confused, and crying hysterically, I asked him why I had to choose—thinking why he would say something this crazy after telling him my secret.

"Dre, look, I need time. I really need to think about this."

I was so sick of people taking advantage of me. So in my mind, I decided it would be on my terms if I gave up my virginity willingly, and I had only a few hours to make that choice because Dre wanted what he wanted. Once he got what he wanted, he treated me as if I was nothing to him.

Meanwhile, Dre started hanging out with the wrong crowd as the months passed. As he neared the end of his senior year and worried about money, he started selling drugs. Eventually, I, too, began indulging in drugs and drinking to get through my days and trying to forget about my pain. More time passed, and I started reflecting on my life. Although I didn't complain about being the girl of a dope dealer and money was flowing like water, I felt uneasy about the pain, risk, and feelings that came with it. But yet, I felt safer with him. I enjoyed spending money on myself and my friends at the mall, driving cars, and having the latest clothes. But the secret kept haunting me. It was constantly in my face, and I finally had to make a decision. Do I continue to live in a house where I'm not protected from abuse or move in with my abusive boyfriend? My life was getting increasingly toxic, yet both options felt comfortable and familiar. My mindset was at least with Dre; I had money and drugs to drown my pain. I spoke to a family member, and her advice was, "If they are paying the bills, then what's the problem?"

Hope felt lost, and I gave up on every fairytale I ever read about growing up. Prince Charming didn't exist in my world. I did not want to live with Dre, so I stayed with my family. I also knew he would take advantage of me at any moment.

Things were getting better with Dre and me. He went six months without putting his hands on me and would ensure I was on time for school. In retrospect, I truly believed I made a great decision.

Then the final straw came!

Dre accused me of cheating on him with his friend. High again, he was looking for a reaction. This time, I didn't give it to him. But my silence made him even more heated. Dre began to beat me worse than the other times. He grabbed my hair and banged my head on the porch. He kicked me in the face and stomach. I broke loose from him and ran into the house to call 911 and my brother.

Hearing yelling outside, I ran to the window and saw Dre pull his gun out, pointing it toward my brother and anyone else there to protect me. I quickly hung up the phone and jumped in front of where the weapon was pointed. I told him he would just have to kill me. He said he didn't want to kill me, and I brought this on myself. If he couldn't be with me, then nobody could. Just as he was about to pull the trigger, the police arrived!

He was taken away without putting up a fight, but fear and questions consumed me. How did the police know the address when I hung up the phone? What is going to happen to me when he gets out? Where am I going to live without fear? Then I heard a knock at the door. Our neighbor, Ms. Brenda said she had enough of him and his mess, so she called the police. It was at that moment I knew God was real.

5

The Cain in My Life

Then the master looked down and saw a vessel of clay. Empty and broken, it helplessly lay. No hope had the vessel that the master might choose to cleanse and make whole, fill and use. "Ah! This is the vessel I've been hoping to find; I will mend and use it and make it all mine. Then gently, he lifted the vessel of clay. HE mended and cleansed it and filled it that day. Spoke to it kindly. You must do work; just pour out to others as I pour into you. – Author Unknown

SOMETIMES OUR FLESH AND blood can be the ones who hurt us the most. This is why we should be careful about who we open our doors to. The bible story of Cain and Abel inspired this chapter as it covers a multitude of relationships. This relationship occurs in many families, friendships, and work environments. Jealousy and envy are works of the flesh; those two topics bring rage, anger, mental instability, and wickedness. I've prayed for many women who have experienced deep trauma but felt muzzled trying to explain their truth. Such fear leads them to protect their offenders.

I, too, was one of those people until more and more women started opening up to me. The more women I saw being silenced due to their past, the angrier I became. I was burning inside, waiting to scream at any woman too afraid to speak up. Most of these women had small children exposed to known abusers because of their loyalty. Yet these women were not strong enough to fight past fear and open their mouths.

Little did I know, as much as I was encouraging them to say something, to stand for something, and be brave, the warrior in me was not ready for battle. I couldn't look at myself in the mirror because the things I expected from them caused a heavy fear in me. Four-year-old Jessica was no longer hidden in deep, inner caverns. She screamed at the top of her lungs for adult Jessica to open her mouth. Yet, I ignored her again. I pushed out the piercing noise with busyness and continued the cycle of leaving her unprotected. The victim became the victimizer.

The first time

"Jessica, come on, hurry up. We are late for church!" My four-year-old self couldn't wait to go to church. My mind imagined those long, comfy pews as my bed. I don't know why I had to go to church; all I did was sleep. Heck, I could sleep in my own bed. Grandma didn't like me sleeping in church but couldn't fuss after me because she sang in the choir. Very faintly, I heard the car starting and took off running outside, so I didn't get left. Grandma! Grandma! Please don't leave me!

"Hurry up, girl."

While in church, the priest told a story about Cain and Abel. My young mind remembered the story like so:

Two brothers Cain was the big brother; Abel was the little brother. Cain killed his little brother, lied about it, and God cursed him for life.[5]

I didn't sleep in the pews this day back then because I was scared that Cain would kill me too, and my imagination was something. After church, we went downstairs to the church hall. They sold Dutch Girl donuts, juice, and coffee. I could not wait for my donut and juice. When I approached the ladies at the table to place my order, I was instantly pulled away and rushed up the basement stairs. My grandma had an emergency with my grandfather on this particular day, so we had to rush back home.

A close family member was at the house and told her he would keep after me while she left. I cried, but she kept walking no matter how loud I got. As my tears dried, I knew something wasn't right, so I went and hid, hoping he would go away. But he didn't. Eventually, I had to use the bathroom.

I tiptoed to the bathroom, thinking I was alone, but as soon as I sat on the toilet, he entered the bathroom, shutting the door behind him. I screamed for him to leave, but he wouldn't. No one was there to protect me. I asked him if he was going to kill me the same way Cain killed Abel in the Bible; he laughed and said, "Only if you tell someone."

That day my innocent little soul became dark. It started a multitude of sexual trauma, which didn't stop for years to come.

Who was the Cain(s) in your life? For me, it came in the form of 12 abusers. By age 15, I had been sexually abused/raped by over 12 men, girls, and boys. I had wounds from incest and non-incest perpetrators. My story is not the first of its kind, nor will it be the last. And yet, just as others before me were brave enough to open their mouths, I will continue to do the same for those who currently feel voiceless.

No one helped me as a child out of the many people who knew my story. This caused me to feel rejected and alone. My heart grew cold, and I barely kept the light of hope. I grew away from the church and no longer came to adults with problems. Life no longer had room for me, and my silence had room to grow as I felt.

I can recall reading the story of a woman named Tamar, daughter of King David. Her half-brother, Amnon, had a very sick, unnatural obsession with her. He lusted over her constantly. One day, he faked a sickness, requesting she fix his food. Once she entered his room, he forced her to have sexual relations with him. She impassively denied it, but he wouldn't take NO for an answer. He raped her, his sister. Tamar ran to her other brother, Absalom, who fruitlessly comforted her. But when her father heard, although angry, he did nothing to protect his daughter. Two years later, Absalom took revenge. Although Absalom had their brother killed, he fled to another place. An act of silence destroyed a family, and all Tamar could do was tear her clothes and walk around with ashes on her forehead.[6]

This story binds the stories of so many of us women, men, and children worthy of protection. Someone abuses us. We tell those who are supposed to protect us, and nothing is done about it. Feelings of rejection, fear, and shame overtake our voices. We become silent and numb. Feelings of being unloved create an atmosphere that allows one's perpetrator to commit their offense repeatedly because you now think no one will care or do anything about it.

6

Choices

Until I finally admitted all my sins to you and stopped trying to hide them. I said, "I will confess them to the Lord." And you forgave me! All my guilt is gone. - Psalm 32:5 TLB

College life

"CAN YOU HEAR ME? Hello...This will do the trick," the emergency room doctor said once I returned to reality. The intense, pungent smell of bleach lingered as I focused on exactly where I was and how I got there.

Quickly glancing to my right, I noticed two close friends sitting in the room. Marian was a short redhead with light brown eyes. She put a twinkle in many guys' eyes, yet tonight she sobbed and reeked of vodka. Nico was of Italian descent, and his olive skin and dark eyes were intensely filled with anger toward me.

The doctor leaned in and said:

"I've witnessed many lives slip away due to addictions. I can tell you are not the first in your family. Because I see many like you week after week, I should report you to the authorities, along with that bar, but I won't. I will allow you to get it right, as your redhead friend will have a conniption if she thinks she has lost you for the second time. I see something inside all three of you, and I hope you each make better decisions."

The doctor left the room to handle some paperwork. As the door closed, Nico's voice instantly became just as loud as a protester on the front line.

"Jessica! What were you and Marian thinking? Had I not found you two in the hallway, Jess would have died. You two drive up my blood pressure."

Marian sobbing even louder as if her dog just died, barely getting her words out, says, "I didn't want to lose my friend, and I know we are too young to drink. I didn't want to take a chance knowing the police could get involved."

Nico was not your typical Italian. He didn't do what other college teens did. Yes, he drank occasionally, but he took his education seriously and honored his family everywhere he traveled. Now standing and pacing the floor,

Nico says, "Jess, you've done it this time." You need to give that stuff up. As your friend, I cannot watch you or Marian throw your lives away. Something has to change. Both of you need to change. Why are you guys like this anyway?"

My heart screamed out loud.

"I am hurting, and I drink to mask my pain. I feel worthless."

But my mouth stayed shut. I could only put my head down in shame. I wished I had the courage to tell someone how I was feeling, but I was too scared. I felt like I was in a dark place, and I didn't know how to get out. I needed help, but I didn't know where to find it. I was so overwhelmed; I just wanted to curl up in a ball and cry. I was so lost and alone.

The sacrifice I never thought I would make

Life became more toxic after Dre. I became really promiscuous. I had no fear of death, no hope for a future with a husband or children. I was lost and drowning in my own choices. This is a challenging subject for many people to discuss because people are on the fence about pro-life or pro-choice. The recent U.S. Supreme Court decision to officially reverse Roe v. Wade declared the constitutional right to abortion no longer exists.[7] Where do I stand now? Right is right, and wrong is wrong.

The Day

The closer I got to the door, the sounds of my heart echoed louder and louder—Dub, dub, dub. Holding back tears, I grabbed the door handle and walked inside the clinic. As I approached the front desk, the receptionist greeted me with a smile.

"Hi, are you here for an appointment?"

Yes, I am.

"Is this your first time visiting with us?"

Yes, ma'am.

"Here, sweetie. Take this and fill out every form to the best of your ability. The nurse will be right with you."

My mind started racing, wondering if I was doing the right thing. Was I going to hell? Would I make it out of the clinic? I started looking around, and I was the only woman in the room with her male companion. I questioned the type of person he was to agree to this with me. I felt embarrassed, alone, and stupid, and I wanted to die with the child.

"Jessica, we're ready for you." Shaking uncontrollably, I stood up to walk, feeling like I had made an appointment with the devil. I thought I had signed a contract with satan, and there was no turning back. Before they could move forward with the procedure, I had to watch a movie about what I was about to do. I had the option to change my mind, yet an intense fear overcame me and turned my stomach upside down.

I was too far in the deep at this point, and the fear of facing family and others was just too much. So, I moved along.

The nurse assigned to me that day performed an ultrasound. I did not want to look because it would give me a lifetime tie to this child, and part of me wanted nothing to do with it.

"Open your eyes and look at the baby. YOUR baby that you are about to terminate."

I didn't want to look, but I turned my head, and tears began falling. I wanted to stop and call everything off, but I didn't want to bring a child into this cold, sick world, especially if the father and I had already rejected it anyway. The room was frigid, the walls were dark, and I felt no warmth or peace.

"Please undress and put on the robe lying on the table. The doctor will be in shortly."

I undressed with tears all over my eyes, regretting my decision and life choices altogether. I lay on the cold table and waited.

Memories of condemnation

There is a process when we think about a wound inflicted by self or others and how to care for it. If the process is not followed correctly, it leaves room for infection and possibly other wounds and scars to appear. This is precisely how condemnation works.

Between 1970 and 2015, there were nearly 45.7 million legally- induced abortions. Sources say abortions are more common in women between the ages of 15 and 44.[8]

I am not proud of my past by any means. By the time I was 20 years old, I had experienced two abortions. Trust me, each time provoked a different reaction. Honestly, I felt relieved after the first abortion. I immediately asked God to forgive me and promised I wouldn't do it again. The first procedure wasn't bad, but the aftermath was horrific. I lost so much blood that I knew I was about to die from what I had just done. Because of this concern, the doctor kept me a little longer under close observation.

The next time was more challenging because I remembered my promise to God. Although I was terrified to tell my family, I was willing to move away and raise the child as a single parent. At the time, the guy I was with was planning to play for a professional sports team, and he wasn't interested in having any kids. Some of his family felt I was trying to get a meal ticket. My father supported my decision to keep the baby, encouraged me, and even spoke to the guy. But the guy was not on board with that plan; most of my other family members weren't either.

There was also a slight fear of having a child that could be molested and taken advantage of like I was, and the thought of bringing a child into such an evil world hurt me. Not to mention, I could not un-hear the following words on replay: "If you get pregnant, I will personally take you to get an abortion, even if I have to borrow the money." And "If you get pregnant, I will kick that baby out of you." Discouraged and defeated, I felt I had no choice. So this time, I went reluctantly. I opted out of seeing the ultrasound because I couldn't handle looking at another one. During this procedure, it wasn't as easy as the first for some reason. I had to push because the baby wasn't coming out. It was awful. The pain was so intense I was mortified. I wanted to stop, but it was too late, and I felt like I had let God down. I felt like an actual murderer and knew I didn't deserve to live. I truly felt I deserved everything terrible that happened to me until now. For years, I carried that secret. I drowned my thoughts and emotions with alcohol and partying. I felt horrible and constantly cried to myself when I saw a baby because of the thoughts going through my mind. I was slightly relieved when the doctors said I could not have children. I felt I didn't deserve any, and if I did, God would punish me for what I had done.

7

The Black Shadow Dream

Be sober-minded; be watchful. Your adversary the devil prowls around like a roaring lion, seeking someone to devour. - 1 Peter 5:8

AFTER PRAYING ONE DAY, I saw this black shadow going back and forth between bedrooms. I became stricken with fear. Later that night, I fell asleep, wondering what that shadow was and how it came into my home.

The dream

Watching from a cracked closet door with full intent, I saw a vast dark shadow wandering about, searching for its next victim. Who will be its dwelling place? The fear over me was like a heavy perfume scent, and I couldn't mask it. The shadow smelled it and began heading my way until my uncle appeared! Fear started crawling up my legs while shaking uncontrollably. Slowly, his wheelchair creeps in, his hair white as snow, and his skin is the perfect blend of a mocha latte with a dab of cream.

It was as if he had misplaced the shadow and was waiting for this very moment to have this encounter. The shadow moved closer, ready to run through the door of fear that I had readily opened. My uncle yelled, "Satan, STOP!"

You have been coming around for fifty-plus years, causing havoc in my mind, family, and spirit. I didn't understand what was happening and why you always loved jumping inside of me. But now, I know who you are and who I am. Satan, you have no place here; you no longer have authority over me or my mind. I won't allow you to control me or those near me a second longer. I command you to go in the mighty name of Jesus. I declare that God's blood is over my family and me. It is written that if I resist you, you will flee. (James 4:7) It is written that the Lord is my shepherd; I shall not want. He makes me lie down in green pastures. He leads me beside still waters. He restores my soul. He leads me in paths of righteousness for his name's sake. Even though I walk through the valley of the shadow of death, I will fear no evil, for Jesus is with me. His rod and staff comfort me. He prepares a table before me in the presence of my enemies; He anoints my head with oil, and my cup overflows.[9] It is written if we confess our sins, HE is faithful and just to forgive us our sins and to cleanse us from all unrighteousness.[10]

Satan, it is written that you must worship the Lord your God, and you must obey him only.[11]

The shadow stood for a second, then flew right out the window. "JE-SUS" is what my uncle shouted after this encounter. I watched as tears dripped from his face, and he began speaking a language only God could understand. He was surrounded by what appeared to be white robes with wings attached, and a feeling of peace was released in the room.

———— ◄O► ————

When I woke up, I thought to myself, "Did God really give me an answer in my dream? Or did I create that, and why was I dreaming about Uncle?" Regardless I had a deep knowing at that moment; I thought I was the only one who had seen the dark shadow moving about daily, searching for its next victim. I had no clue what that shadow was doing, but I was driven to pray a prayer of protection when I saw it, and it felt good I was not the only one who saw a dark shadow. Freedom, Strength, and Wisdom are what I witnessed in that dream. My next mission was to seek answers from my great uncle.

8

Groundhog Day

Unforgiveness is like drinking poison yourself and waiting for the other person to die. - Marianne Williamson

HAVE YOU EVER ASKED someone for forgiveness, but they didn't forgive you? Do you remember the pain you felt? The rejection was so heartbreaking that you may have replayed the scenario repeatedly in your head, trying to think about what you could've done differently. Then you start thinking about all the times that person messed up, and you could've forgiven them on numerous occasions.

Unforgiveness can be a nasty theme when we repeatedly play this hurtful game. If someone offends me, I won't offer forgiveness. If I hurt someone, I feel entitled to their forgiveness. As humans, our feelings are valid in most cases and yet fickle. They change often; for the most part, we are not objective in our views and thoughts of situations close to home. God is not like us. He sees and knows all things. He accepts us when we ask for forgiveness. When we are genuinely sorry about what we've done in our hearts, God forgives us and forgets. He doesn't bring it up with every argument, disagreement, or bad day. He won't throw what you or I did in our faces when we are doing well to bring us down, nor does He throw things in our faces when you or I are at our lowest. He will not condemn you or me if we repeat our offenses. There are consequences and corrections within all situations, both good and bad.

For years I allowed myself to walk around wounded and angry, replaying the traumas I experienced and the roles I played in my life, good, bad, and indifferent. Unforgiveness was clothed in addictions, resentment, laughter, and deep trust issues. My words and mind whispered,

"Jessica, you are free. You are healed." But deep down in my soul, I knew I wasn't. I was a mess and felt like this wound could never be healed. My wound was deep, and I'm sure some of you reading this chapter have felt the same at some point. Listen, I get it, Forgiveness takes time, but it also takes action. There is hope for you and me. I am here to share a story about how one woman took my broken, wounded self and spoke life into me without ever meeting me. Through her obedience, my life was changed forever.

———◦———

One night while lying in bed, my television was on, and a woman started to share her testimony of how she experienced years of rape and molestation from her biological father. She explained how her mother knew what was happening and did nothing about it. This lady went on with her tragic story and formed her mouth to say God told her to forgive them! She proceeded to say that not only did she have to forgive them, but since they were up in age, she also had to move them closer to her and take care of them. After three years of her parents living in their new home, her dad finally apologized for what he did to her. She placed her arm around him and told him she had forgiven him years ago. That same day her dad prayed the prayer of salvation with her and her husband. He then asked his daughter to baptize him![12]

This testimony woke me straight up. What in tarnation did this lady say? My heart started racing, and my mind flooded with thoughts. There was no way the God I knew and studied would tell someone to do such a crazy thing! I just knew this lady was crazy and lying through her teeth. I couldn't be the only person thinking this lady was off her rocker. But sisters, guess what? She wasn't; matter of fact, she was saner than I was. This woman understood a few things I did not:

- God's ways are not our ways.

- She knew God intimately, and I can honestly say I did not.

- Forgiveness brings about peace; peace is a choice, not a law.

- Forgiveness is the secret to healing many wounds.

With tears streaming down my face, the more she talked, the more healing I felt. Messages resonate deep in your soul differently when you can relate to someone who has been through similar situations. You understand the pain and the depth of the wound. To hear how God healed this woman gave me hope. To see how the generational issues of silence, of dealing with incest and all its attachments, could be broken from her family and hundreds of thousands of others, myself and you included. I witnessed the power of God that day. I saw the power of Story and Truth. I witnessed God as a healer. Joyce Meyer and her testimony started me on a journey of healing and a relationship with God. I took God's word and put action to it, even if it meant forgiving the hard things. Meyer was the first person I heard break down scriptures in a way that made sense. She tackled real-life issues honestly.

———◦———

Can you recall hearing others in and out of church talking about forgiveness? We often hear, "If you truly forgive someone, you forget the offense." That was the craziest and most challenging thing to wrap my head around. My thought was, "HOW?" Deep down in my heart, I often cried myself to sleep and thought I was going to hell because I couldn't forget. So by its own logic, I did not truly forgive. As a child, innocent minds take things like this for face value, and when I was a child, I took people's words literally. Yet, none of the people going around quoting forgive and forget ever showed me how. And if actions spoke louder than words, I had no map or direction to follow. Simply, their words left me lost and confused.

C.S. Lewis once said, "Everyone says forgiveness is a lovely idea until they have something to forgive." Let that sit in your spirit for a minute. How often have we been so quick to defend ourselves, wanting others to forgive us for our justified actions? But reverse roles and place the shoe on the other foot, we sift through all the facts with a fine-tooth comb. Now, I'm not in any way minimizing anyone's actions. We know when wrong is wrong. I'm simply wondering why don't we extend the same grace to others. Why is forgiving so complicated and complex? Do we truly know how to forgive? Why do we replay situations repeatedly until it becomes our internal mental personal number-one hit TV show?

We have replayed situations in our minds so much we have already come up with different outcomes and scenarios on why we shouldn't forgive. Our actions lead us down a path of self-isolation and silence, which compounds deeper wounds. We feed the hurt, doing everything to keep it alive. Much like in the 1993 movie, "Groundhog Day," the main character repeatedly lives out the same day. The difference between us and the movie; is the film lasts an hour and 41 minutes, while our reality is not promised tomorrow.[13] At what point will we decide enough is enough? Our lives are far too meaningful to allow our healing to be contingent upon someone else's life choices.

9

Not Worthy of Motherhood

And the LORD was gracious to Hannah; she gave birth to three sons and two daughters. Meanwhile, the boy Samuel grew up in the presence of the LORD. - 1 Samuel 2:21 (NIV)

ON A COLD WINTER night in early 2009, my husband and I were home in our 900-square-foot, 2-bedroom apartment. I don't quite remember what led to this, but we walked from our living room to our bedroom, and I immediately laid my hands on my husband's back as he knelt before the Lord, and I was led to pray for him. As I prayed, the Lord showed me a vision to share with him. Immediately after telling him what I saw about him, I heard the Lord say to me clear as day. "You will bear a son and call him Joshua."

I was confused as to why God would speak to me about a son; I felt I was not worthy of motherhood. Part of me thought I was hearing things, but the other part trusted every word. God knew I could not mentally birth a daughter first, so I believed the voice.

At the time, my husband and I had been married for almost a year, and sometime later started planning for our first child. In the beginning stages, my menstrual cycle would come and go. This happened for a few months, so naturally, I assumed I was the problem.

The memories from the abortions and my health issue from four years prior began to haunt me.

Effects of birth control

It was the second semester of my first year of college. I started forgetting to take my birth control, so I decided to try a newer, more effective method known as the Patch. This birth control resembles a square Band-Aid and is placed on your skin to help prevent your ovaries from releasing eggs. Shortly after starting this Patch, I had a sharp abdominal pain that caused me to curl over as if being punched in the stomach. I experienced many tears in my eyes. The nonstop pain didn't ease after taking pain medication. After waiting a few hours, the pain wouldn't disappear. I went to the campus clinic to discover the reason for the problem. At first, the doctor was worried about the possibility of a tubal pregnancy. But I assured her I had not been sexually active. However, to cover her bases, she ran a test to rule out pregnancy. Later, she wrote my symptoms off as bad premenstrual cramps. Gave me pain meds, and I returned to my dorm room.

Later that night, I walked into the bathroom, then... the pain began to increase to a level so excruciating I was left in a somewhat paralyzed state. I couldn't move, but I was able to scream before collapsing on the bathroom floor. Terrified because I was now bleeding as if I was on my period, throwing up, and too weak even to clean myself. Those screams saved my life as my roommate and suitemates ran to get help from our Resident Advisor (RA). And though my friend Shawn came to help me, I can't remember all the details, except he drove me to the local hospital.

While at the hospital, the doctors checked me by taking an ultrasound of my ovaries and lower abdomen area and drawing blood. They also connected me to an IV and gave me a shot in my buttocks for the pain. After reviewing my test, the doctors came in and said that I was suffering from a severe ovarian cyst. They explained to me that my cyst was the size of a golf ball and the pain I was feeling was because it had ruptured inside of me. Due to its size, the toxins and bleeding could be poisonous enough to kill me.[14]

The doctors were ready to rush me to surgery for an emergency hysterectomy. The nurse called my mother, and she gave them the green light to go ahead because they told her it would save my life! I spoke to my mom and told her I wasn't going to go along with it. I felt that it had to be another way to fix this issue. I refused the surgery, yet they kept trying to push it on me. Still lying in the hospital bed connected to an IV, I looked at Shawn and said: "Break me out of here NOW!"

He did just that. I disconnected my IV; Shawn helped me grab my clothes and broke me out of that hospital!

Still in much pain, laying across the back seat for three hours, he took me home to my mom in Detroit, MI, where I stayed the weekend until I felt a little better. My mom tried convincing me I would have been ok had I had the surgery. But for me, an 18-year-old female getting a hysterectomy was both unheard of and just crazy in my mind. Whether I wanted children or not, I wanted it to be on my terms. I felt there was an underlining agenda as to why the doctors would like to perform a complete hysterectomy on me, and I wasn't about to be their practice dummy.

I suffered from severe, ongoing ovarian cysts monthly after that first encounter. I also stopped using The Patch as birth control. The cyst would rupture monthly, and I would deal with them as they came for four years. Every month, the pain would be the same: I would need assistance from friends and family in helping me get dressed, use the bathroom, clean myself and walk. When I didn't have help, I would just lay in the bathroom until I could crawl and pull myself together.

2005

A year later, while back home in Detroit, MI attending Community College and working, I was still dealing with an ongoing ovarian cyst issue. As usual, I went for my yearly pap smear exam, and I didn't think twice about it. After a day or two, I received a call saying that my "results came back abnormal. The doctors would like to do further testing." Still not feeling alarmed, I went back for re-testing. When the results came back, I was told I had pre-cancerous cells on my cervix. I was informed I may never be able to have children and further testing needed to be done. I felt as though I couldn't catch a break. Why am I dealing with all this crap from these doctors? Why is God punishing me?

Growing up, I dealt with abuse, from sexual to physical. It is not something I'm proud of or wear as a badge of honor. But it's critical to understand my journey. These things left me in a state of depression, unworthiness, and brokenness. My thoughts stayed on why me and not the Lord. I made my mind up as a young teenager that the good people in this world existed few and far between. For that matter, this world was nowhere for a child to be born, primarily through me. Marriage would never be an option in my future as I had too much baggage and trust issues, and the probability of becoming a single mother, I felt, was high. But yet again, the choice of being able to have a child should be mine and not these doctors'.

The big day came a few weeks after my last follow-up. The doctors performed a colposcopy[15] and cervical biopsy.[16] I signed a release form from the hospital to allow my procedure to be recorded for study purposes. As I entered the hospital room to undress, my nerves, faith, and thoughts roamed everywhere, and all I could think about was, "What am I doing here? How did I get to this point where I'm constantly hospitalized? What if I die young from cancer? What if this is it? What do I have to show for my life?"

With a million more questions in my head, I silently walked down the hall, escorted by a nurse to the exam room where the procedure would take place. I lay in bed waiting for the doctors to arrive.

They shot me with a needle to numb me for the procedures. They inserted a tool with a video camera attachment into my cervix, and BAM! Just like that, all those tiny white dots were in front of my eyes on the

TV screen. The doctor said he could freeze them and they should go away. They could go away on their own, which means the recommended treatment was to monitor the situation with more frequent Pap tests every six months, or lastly worst-case scenario, the cells could turn into full-blown cancer. Either way, be OK with possibly being unable to have children.

I trusted and believed in God for healing all over my body. I went to the elder women in the church for prayer. They interceded on my behalf, and I prayed over myself. That following year, those pre-cancerous cells were ALL gone, and I was on medication to help with the cyst problem.

> "Therefore, I tell you, whatever you ask in prayer, believe that you have received it, and it will be yours." - Mark 11:24

Back to 2009

I had recently come off the medicine controlling the cyst. I returned to the doctor and was told I was as fertile as a rabbit! Well, what could be the problem? I started looking at my husband and suggested (or I may have driven him) he go to the doctor to get checked out. There were no issues there as well. I gave up trying, and then.... July 2009, this happened!

I couldn't believe it; I was pregnant! I knew it was Joshua in my womb! People thought I was crazy! But I never forgot what the Lord told me. What a blessing to be a part of such a time when the Lord Himself saw fit for my husband and me to become parents to Joshua! But not without a cost.

The cost

Nine months later, I was now in active labor with Joshua for two days; at this point, I was tired and in much pain. The doctor kept sending me home even though my contractions were real and frequent, but I had not dilated enough.

"Go home and walk until you can't walk anymore," she said.

Well, I did just that! I walked and walked and walked until I literally could not walk anymore. With my husband and sister Leah right by my side, I walked (well, they carried me) into the hospital. I was admitted and told I'll be kept overnight for monitoring. If they decided to induce me, I would have time to let everyone know. Thinking everything was normal and well, I sent my husband home (against his better judgment) to finish drying the clothes. He felt he needed to stay, but I insisted he leave. My sister Leah, a high-school junior at the time, was with us, so I figured she would call him if there were a problem or if I needed anything. My husband kissed me and reiterated how crazy it was for him to leave, but he did. He called me when he got home to check on Josh and me. I reassured him all was well, and a nice older nurse was setting up an IV to help control my contractions overnight. We hung up, and death was staring me in my eyes!

The nurse successfully inserts the IV and goes through the flushing part.

She made small talk with both my sister Leah and me. Then she asked:

"Have you ever had Novocain before?"

I answered, No, ma'am.

The nurse told me the medicine she was about to put in my IV was like Novocaine. She said it would numb me and ease my contractions overnight. She insisted that it was safe for both the baby and me. Fearful again, I looked her in her eyes, then looked down at the small brown medicine bottle and said, OK.

Imagine lying in a hospital bed, 39 weeks and five days pregnant, experiencing contractions for three days straight. You are in so much pain it hurts to walk. Fear is showing all over your face, and you put 100% of your trust in the medical staff to help with the agony. Then, you are given medicine through an IV to help make you comfortable. But you start to gasp for air. Trying to tell the nurse you can't breathe; instead of helping you, she sits and watches you turn red, screaming for help. Your sister is yelling, "SHE CAN'T BREATHE!" over and over. The nurse stands up, slides the medicine into her left pocket, writes down some notes, and walks out of the room, leaving you for dead, never mentioning a thing to anyone!

Scared and nervous, my sister ran into the hallway, screaming and yelling for help. That was my last memory before falling into a deep sleep. It was peaceful, and I had no clue that my son and I FLAT LINED together.

10

The Wall

Have I not commanded you? Be strong and courageous. Do not be afraid; do not be discouraged, for the LORD your God will be with you wherever you go.- Joshua 1:9 (NIV)

I REMEMBER WHEN I was a young child; many things did not scare me. Things any average child would be afraid of, such as darkness and scary movies, gave me a sense of peace. Partly because my father had a Freddy Krueger costume, and I thought he played the character. I understood my Dad to be a funny, trustworthy, and loving person, so naturally, I assumed there was nothing to be afraid of; until I learned the truth. When my little self found out the man in the movie was not my Dad acting, I was confused and mortified. Fear entered my heart faster than a speeding bullet.

Over the years, I noticed myself becoming fearful of almost everything. A once brave young girl who found peace in the dark now ran up the stairs, panicking and looking behind her because the fun, scary movies also taught her to do crazy things when afraid. I was pretty much a "hot mess." It was so bad if I was at a restaurant and people looked at me while I was eating; I would either not eat or have my food packed to go. As I grew older, so did my fears. I went from being free-spirited, wanting to bungee jump, jet ski, and skydive, to fearing thunder, heights, bridges, water, boats, and the like. Yet, the thought of my death and God scared me not.

———•◦•———

As a media major in college, I had to write and act. Writing was easy, but acting in front of a camera or delivering speeches was an entirely different ballgame. I recall when my professor asked me to give a speech:

"Jessica, I've pushed your speech off until the last day; please stand in front of the class and deliver your assignment; it's 60% of your final grade."

All I could remember is everything around me was a blur. I stood up and started walking to the front of the class with my head down. Embarrassment was an understatement, and I was terrified. The palms of my hands were sweaty, and an urge to use the bathroom came over me. My heart started fluttering fast, and my legs and hands shook uncontrollably. When I lifted my head to start speaking, I felt fear standing behind me. It had my mouth muzzled, and I was fighting to get my words out. But I couldn't; fear was winning, and no one could help me. So, I cried. Tear after tear dripped down my face and onto my note cards. My professor didn't know to laugh or feel sorry for me. My classmates knew me enough to know I needed help, and one spoke up for me. But my professor was over my shenanigans, and I was sent to the Dean's office.

A quick plan was created after telling the Dean what happened and about my extreme fear of speaking. My Dean talked to my professor and made an exception for me. I was still fully responsible for delivering my speech, but this time facing the wall, without having to look at anyone face to face. My body kept the score with fear, and I had no clue.

———•◦•———

Battlefield of the mind

I once read a quote by John Milton: "The mind is its place and, in itself, can make a heaven of Hell, a hell of Heaven." On many occasions, I've witnessed myself and others permit a door called "worry." That door, once opened, causes havoc in our minds. One day while sitting on the couch, I received a phone call, and the mere sight of this person's name sent me into a frenzy. My heart fluttered rapidly, my ears closed, and I only heard "dub, dub, dub...." My throat began to close up, and the feeling of needing air grew. I felt as if I was drowning underwater, and my fingers became tingly. As sweat dripped from my face down my neck, I quickly closed my eyes, took a few deep breaths, and turned my phone on do not disturb.

That feeling went away after about 10/11 seconds. I thought I was fine, but the feeling persisted when that person and another would call. I couldn't recall ever experiencing such a feeling before in my life. This feeling began to grow more intense. I had to contact my doctor.

While at my checkup, I explained to him what happened recently. His response was:

"I would like to monitor you closely for a couple of weeks. Although, I strongly believe you are indeed experiencing full-blown panic attacks. But here is the thing, because you are pregnant, there isn't much I can do for you right now. You can naturally get through the attacks and keep them 30 seconds and below. So I believe you can overcome this. In the meantime, I suggest removing those people from your daily life."

I left the doctor that day with high hopes of beating this thing, yet in the back of my mind, I constantly wondered where this issue came from. When did this start? I couldn't understand why this was happening to me, nor would I give up until I found the answer I sought.

Part II

HEALING
PAST ——◆•◆—— WOUNDS

"Your Wound was probably not your fault, but your healing is your responsibility." - Denice Frohman

II

A Time To Grieve

The Lord is near to the brokenhearted and saves the crushed in spirit. - Psalm 34:18 NIV

WHILE GRIEVING THE LOSS of my grandmother, I had to be completely honest with myself. I was in the middle of a season where I was intentionally seeking God, searching for something more in life, and figuring out who I was. I was too weak to face this journey head-on, alone and sober-minded. I used my grandmother's death to enable my negative habits further. I used my emotions to seek things outside of God. Dealing with such a rough moment, I could not see myself living without her. I could not see how people dealt with death through Jesus. I did everything to suppress my feelings and very little to face them and allow myself to heal.

Losing a loved one is never easy to deal with, whether they are an infant or 110 years old. Although we all understand death is the only thing guaranteed in life, not one of us is promised tomorrow. Yet, we respond to death like most of us opening a can of biscuits: shocked and fearful, as if we didn't know that pop was going to happen. Of course, we want to control the outcome, but that's not our job. My grandmother's passing made me finally acknowledge where I was mentally, emotionally, spiritually, and physically.

I attended a funeral for another family member, and I can recall the pastor saying something along the lines of "This person had a birth date and a death date, but what they did during the period of that dash in the middle is what mattered." I realized that day I was spending my dash mourning, grieving, and having pity parties. I was not living, and if I died that day, I don't think God would've said, "Good job, my good and faithful servant." The Bible tells us in Ecclesiastes 3:1-4 NIV:

> There is a time for everything and a season for every activity under the heavens: a time to be born and a time to die, a time to plant and a time to uproot, a time to kill and a time to heal, a time to tear down and a time to build, a time to weep and a time to laugh, a time to mourn and a time to dance.

This means God knows we will mourn and gives us time to do so. When we allow ourselves to mourn and grieve for far too long, we start to lose all hope. God does not want that for us. He wants us to heal. This means surrendering to Him. I had to face the truth, and my reality was I idolized my grandmother. I depended on her so much I didn't know how to live without her. I felt that living my life without staying in a place of sadness would mean I had moved on and she was no longer a part of me, and I thought it meant I would forget her. Internally, I had accepted her death spiritually and knew she was ready to go. My healing took time, and I mean a lot, and I had to push myself day by day.

Have you ever grieved a loved one? Did you ever have peace in your heart? Maybe, you never grieved losing someone to death. Perhaps it was a friendship, your innocence, a divorce, a job, an animal, or your old self. Whatever it is, know that Jesus heals. By His stripes, you are healed according to His word. You do not have to stay in a place of sadness. He wants you to embrace love, joy, and peace.

The healing process

We must understand that it's a process to heal from grief. It's normal to experience many emotions. Grief does not discriminate by sex, age, or race. Science shows that we experience five stages of grief: denial, anger, bargaining, depression, and acceptance.[17] If you can be honest with yourself, I encourage you to write where you are in the process. Write how you feel. Ask God to help you. And to show you what steps you should take next. For me, it was keeping a journal, having a solid support system, seeking wise counsel, and spending time around people who would encourage and pray for me. Next, I had to pay attention to my overall health and move from a place of denial. Finally, I had to open the door and allow God and others to love me through each stage.

Let's heal and overcome

In a journal, write down the names of who or what you're still grieving. Take a breath. Inhale slowly and exhale slowly. Repeat this a few times and release it all. Find some scriptures on comfort and allow that to be your focus on the day.

Connecting with others and finding someone you can confide in during this season of your life can help keep you moving forward and not feeling lonely. Consider sharing happy memories as well.

Get out of the house! Going on walks, relaxing at the beach, dancing, and laughing helped my healing process.

What are you going to do with your dash? Will you let it die with who or what you are grieving? Will you choose to live and allow God to heal you and give you purpose?

———◦———

Pray

Father, Your word says You heal the brokenhearted and bind their wounds. So today, God, I'm asking that You bind up mine. I surrender my grief and every heavy burden to You. I ask that You allow me to be whole in You. Allow me to not be vain in my grief but to grieve well. Father, Your word says blessed are those who mourn, for they shall be comforted. Bring me comfort during the midnight hour and the day. Bring me comfort when I am overcome with memories that are not of joy and peace. Please help me accept what I cannot change and walk in a peace that surpasses all understanding. Father, I ask that You be my strength, have mercy on me, O God. In Jesus' name, I pray. Amen.

What's T.R.U.?

Yes, it's true. I have experienced grief in my life. It's hard to move forward. My heart hurts, and I just can't shake the feeling. It's never-ending. Feelings of hopelessness, pain, anger, anxiousness, rejection, and loneliness overcome me. How could God let this happen?

What's Truth?

God's Word says: "He will wipe every tear from their eyes. There will be no more death or mourning or crying or pain, for the old order of things has passed away." (Revelation 21:4 BSB)

"Why, my soul, are you downcast? Why so disturbed within me? Put your hope in God, for I will yet praise him, my Savior and my God." (Psalm 42:5 NIV)

"For his anger lasts only a moment, but his favor lasts a lifetime! Weeping may last through the night, but joy comes with the morning." (Psalm 30:5 NLT)

12

No Longer Bound To Trauma

Silence about trauma also leads to death-the death of the soul. - Bessel Van Der Kolk, M.D.

TRAUMA USUALLY OCCURS WHEN a person is overwhelmed by events or circumstances and responds with intense fear, horror, and helplessness. Extreme stress overwhelms the person's capacity to cope. There is a direct correlation between trauma and physical health conditions such as diabetes, COPD, heart disease, cancer, and high blood pressure.[18]

Your trauma wound(s) may not have been from physical or sexual abuse. Its root cause may have come from:

Childhood abuse;

Spiritual or emotional abuse;

Natural disasters, an accident, pandemic trauma;

Medical diagnosis, grief, loss, war;

Cultural injustice, your DNA, or from witnessing harm to others.

However you have been affected along your journey, I want you to know, I'm truly sorry this happened to you. No one deserves to walk around wounded and unhealed from any form of trauma. But I do want to encourage you; as long as you're still breathing, you are capable of choosing to heal. You are not broken beyond repair. Those traumatic moments wounded you, but God's word says he is near the brokenhearted. Jesus wants us to surrender our burdens to him and no longer carry the weight of our trauma. Nevertheless, I am certain I can write an entire book on those traumas alone. But sticking with the wounds I touched on earlier, let's further discuss those.

Sexual trauma

Sexual and physical abuse is swept under the rug by families worldwide, leaving women and men alike wounded from their past due to trauma. In most cases, I find those who are supposed to protect us, such as parents, police officers, pastors, teachers, and (fill in the blank____), are not equipped to help us. They, too, may have been unprotected products of abuse. Most times, it's generational, and because they may never have received proper healing to help keep you safe or guide you through your journey, your trauma story either:

Triggers their story, and they are not ready to face it yet.

You are the product of rape or incest, a constant reminder.

Your caregiver was or is dependent on that person for their livelihood.

They are too weak to open their mouths.

They never loved you to begin with.

Drugs or alcohol play a huge role in their lives.

Fill in the blank: _____

In the book "The Body Keeps The Score: Brain, Mind, And Body in The Healing of Trauma," Bessel Van Der Kolk, M.D. gives a great example:

"If you hide from yourself that an uncle molested you when you were young, you are vulnerable to react to triggers like an animal in a thunderstorm: with a full-body response to the hormones that signal "danger." Without language and context, your awareness may be limited. If you keep secrets and suppress information, you are fundamentally at war with yourself. Hiding your feelings can sap life right out of you. Leaving you stressed out, unmotivated, with headaches, body and muscle aches, problems with your bowels and sexual functions, irrational behaviors that hurt you and people around you."

Can you recall moments in your life where you could respond yes to any of the following:

Unwilling to be left alone with certain people. Afraid to be away from primary caregivers, especially if this is a new behavior.

Regressive or resuming behaviors you have grown out of.

Thumb-sucking or bedwetting.

Overly compliant behavior.

Spending an unusual amount of time alone.

Feeling shame and guilt.

Feeling numb to abuse.

Feeling silenced and voiceless.

Keeping more secrets than usual, not talking much.

Feeling fearful.

Finding it difficult to trust others.

Wearing oversize clothes to hide your body.

Physical Abuse

I know many of you are probably wondering what happened to Dre and me. After the police arrived, Dre was handcuffed and taken to the local police station, where he was held for a couple of days. He called my phone back-to-back, leaving threatening messages each time. The operator would say, "You have a collect call from; you better pick up this MF'ing phone." or "I'm sorry, please answer." I never knew if it was going to be Dr. Jekyll or Mr. Hyde.[19] However, I knew I feared for my life.

The detective on this case called me and insisted that I came to the station and file a Police Protection Order (PPO) against him. I told her I was scared, and she assured me I would be OK. So, my brother Chris and our cousin Willie took me to the precinct. I filed the paperwork and came clean to my family about what had been happening all along.

My Godmother served him the paperwork some days later. I was still triggered every time I saw him in the neighborhood or as he drove by.

Months later, Dre called me and reached out to apologize. I was not having it, but something just seemed different, so I obliged and met up with him anyway. One time turned into many, and I truly believed he was a changed man. Yet, deep down, I knew something wasn't right with what we were doing. So, I gave him a call and mustered up enough strength to end this toxic back and forth and sneaking around. I forgave him and moved on with my life to another toxic relationship. Except this time, I knew I was worth more and didn't deserve to be abused by another man. So I ended that relationship and let the police handle the situation moving forward.

I was just like many other broken women when I was with Dre. I made a lot of mistakes and felt too weak to move on. I felt I could be the one to change him. I also feared him more than God, and as a coping mechanism, I developed a toxic trust and deep affection for many of my abusers, known as Stockholm Syndrome.

If you have ever been in or witnessed someone in a physically abusive situation, can you recall moments in your life where you could respond yes to any of the following:

- Developing a deeper love or bond with your abuser;

- Having a desire to protect them;

- Blaming yourself for your abuse;

- Using make-up to cover the scars;

- Isolating yourself from friends and family;

- Having a fear of retaliation if you tell others;

- Making excuses for toxic verbal abuse;

- Financially dependent on the abuser, or they solely control finances in the household without discussion;

- Feelings of pressure to perform sexual acts or forced to use substances;

- Your abuser insulting your parenting skills and threatening to take away or harm your children and or pets;

- Your abuser has actively vandalized your property and or belongings?

No one deserves to experience any type of abuse, but by being truthful and honest about where we are, we can start our healing journey. Whichever the case may be, God no longer wants trauma to be the focus of your story. God wants you healed! He wants you to release those people and offenses. Harboring unforgiveness will keep you from walking in wholeness. God wants to use you for His Glory and to help others heal from this wound. This is not excusing your abuser. What they did to you was dead wrong. But forgiveness frees a piece of you so you can break generational cycles and focus entirely on your healing and the mission to which God has called you.

Let's heal and overcome

If you have ever been a victim of physical abuse, rape, molestation, or incest, understand it was not your fault. If you were a child victim, you might have wondered why other adults didn't help or notice. The Rape, Abuse, and Incest National Network (RAINN) website offers information and support for individuals and families. Encapsulated in their website reveals the truth we may overlook:

"When someone outside the family abuses a child, the child's family can often offer support and a sense of safety. When the abuser is someone in the family, the family may be unable to provide support or a sense of safety."

This information opened my eyes and gave me a sense of peace. I realized I could no longer hold others accountable for my healing. Many of my wounds were not healed as a child because I was raised by generations of unhealed individuals trying to get through life themselves. Ill-equipped, they could not give the tools needed to heal. We have to acknowledge we can't carry their wounds nor change their journey, but we can admit what T.R.U was (Trauma, Rejection & Unforgiveness) for us personally at that moment:

For me:

1. I was sexually and physically abused and rejected.

2. I carried unforgiveness and harbored trust issues.

3. I chose rebellion and looked to drugs and alcohol to get through each day.

4. I was embarrassed that I had allowed myself to stay in an abusive relationship.

5. I lived with hate and anger in my heart.

6. I wanted to feel truly loved, so I looked in all the wrong places.

7. I became depressed and felt shame, disgust, and dirty.

8. I wore clothes that hid my body to make myself less appealing.

9. I smiled daily because my internal pain was too much to bear and face.

10. I got piercings and tattoos because the pain satisfied me for a small moment.

As I just shared several T.R.U. confessions of mine, I invite you to grab a pen and write several of your own.

1.

2.

3.

4.

5.

6.

7.

8.

9.

10.

I find writing to be a very effective tool in the healing process. Writing allows for a great deal of unconfinement and vulnerability. No one is there to reject or ridicule you. Just you, your pen, and God. This exercise won't heal your wounds overnight but will help the process. I recommend asking for help. Trauma, especially sexual and physical trauma, can be tough to deal with. Seeking a therapist or counselor specializing in this area can help you heal. Speak out and share your testimony with others you can trust. Being able to say aloud to a safe person, "I was raped," "My spouse abused me," or "My parents abused me and called it discipline." Naming your wounds, whether big or small, offers a better possibility as you take back your life.

In the book of Genesis, Adam was in charge of the animal kingdom, and his first act was to give a name to every living creature. When you think about your situation, naming those wounds paves a new road leading to forgiving yourself and fully articulating your thoughts, emotions, and complex feelings. You need people who will take your story before the Lord and pray for and with you. Maybe join a small prayer group focusing on sisterhood and healing. Or maybe go out and create what hasn't been created for you and others. Take care of yourself by being mindful of your thoughts, words, habits, and actions. This will connect you to your triggers and when you need help. This is so important as it better enables you to verbalize what you need at that moment instead of assuming others should know.

Pray

Father God, in the name of Jesus, I ask that You free me from this infirmity, guilt, fear, pain, shame, trauma, and brokenness. Heal me from the (i.e.: incest, molestation, physical, spiritual, and psychological abuse or rape) that I have experienced in my lifetime. I decree and declare that the abuse I have suffered will not keep me bound; it will no longer cripple me or bring condemnation. I command the wounds and the effects of sexual abuse and everything connected to it to come up out of me right now in the name of Jesus. Father, I thank You that strongholds and generational curses will be broken from my family and me. Lord, as I begin to heal, I ask to be set free and delivered. Father, I ask You to recover the little child inside me and heal the teenager and the adult. I pray You will guide me, Father, and let Your Spirit rest upon my heart. Let my flesh die to itself and increase Your Spirit in me, Father. Father God, I forgive myself; forgive my abuser/ abusers. May they come to You in repentance. Father, I pray You will heal my mind, soul, spirit, and heart in a powerful way so I will not hold onto these hurts and memories but release them to You. O Lord, as I let go of the burdens and pain. I pray You will begin to do a mighty work in me. Father, I speak life, love, freedom, and wholeness over myself and the generations after me. In the name of Jesus, I pray. Amen.

What's T.R.U.?

Yes, you may have experienced trauma. It hurt, creating a wound so deep the pain of healing was just as hard. You may have thought your recovery meant your abusers were off the hook. But it was indeed the very opposite.

What's Truth?

God's Word says: "The Lord tests the righteous, but his soul hates the wicked and the One who loves violence." (Psalm 11:5)

"Therefore, confess your sins to one another and pray for one another, that you may be healed. The prayer of a righteous person has great power as it is working." (James 5:16)

"But now, God's Message,

the God who made you in the first place, Jacob,

the One who got you started, Israel:

"Don't be afraid; I've redeemed you.

I've called your name. You're mine.

I'll be there with you when you're over your head.

When you're in rough waters, you will not go down.

When you're between a rock and a hard place,

it won't be a dead end—

Because I am God, your personal God,

The Holy of Israel, your Savior.

I paid a huge price for you:

All of Egypt, with rich Cush and Seba thrown in!

That's how much you mean to me!

That's how much I love you!

I'd sell off the whole world to get you back,

trade the creation just for you." (Isaiah 43:1-4 MSG)

13

No More Black Shadow

It is only in our darkest hours that we may discover the true strength of the brilliant light within ourselves that can never, ever be dimmed. – Doe Zantamata

MY GREAT-UNCLE SIDNEY STRUGGLED with a form of depression called Bipolar-Schizophrenia Disorder. His battle with depression began years before I was born. I remember watching him go off the grid every October around Halloween, and I never understood why. Some speculated it was because his mother, my maternal great-grandmother, passed away around that time.

Nevertheless, my story begins in 2009 when I was thrown into the role of his power of attorney. Initially, I felt having that much decision-making power and trust was a huge burden. I felt too young for such a heavy responsibility. Anyone of my many fantastic family members could've taken on this role with much more experience and ease. But, to my dismay, I was chosen.

Caring for someone with a mental illness

Other family members could recall the worst-case stories about Great-Uncle Sidney, but I was never exposed to that person. It was like the person they spoke of never existed around me. Yes, he confirmed many of their tales, but I never met that version of him.

One day my great aunt and other relatives were done with my uncle's shenanigans, and I was called to intervene. He only wanted to talk to my husband and me. That night, we eventually took him to the hospital. After a few days of evaluations, he was sent to a rehabilitation center. I constantly had to make tough decisions in my hard conversations with my uncle. With each blow he was given, his soul slowly drifted into a deep depression. Yes, he was in his right mind and could walk around freely at the rehab. So, I would pick him up and take him to family events, out to eat, and run errands. We spent a lot of time together.

Once his time was up at rehab, a decision had to be made about his living arrangements. He decided to become a full-time resident in the nursing home section of the building. Although I was power of attorney, my uncle still made his own decisions. That included going out drinking and smoking with other family members and staff at his living place. Oh, did he have a blast! Yet, in all the fun, I watched his health decline more and more. At each late-night party he attended, I would receive calls from the emergency department at the nearby hospital, followed up with calls from the nursing home, state social workers, and anyone else involved in my uncle's care. Leaving my family in the middle of the night while looking for someone to watch our children became harder and harder. But as his money started to run out and his ability to walk on his own, friend and family visits became nonexistent for a while. The happy smiles at the mention of his name became like a burden to others. They no longer had use for him. My cousin and I became the ones responsible for his health and well-being. Yet, I still had to make the final decisions and deliver all the good and bad news every time.

My uncle noticed how the outings stopped, and visits slowed down from others. He was quickly falling back into depression. His heart hurt from grief. He grieved the loss of family and his dear cat, Irene. He grieved his old way of living.

One day while in prayer, I felt a strong urge to visit my uncle before the day passed. I noticed he wasn't eating when I arrived at his room. I asked him if he wanted me to get him something else, and he said: "I'm going to just starve myself and die. My sisters and brother are gone, and close cousins, friends, cat, and ex-wife are gone. And I can't walk. What do I have to live for? I just want God to take me, hell!"

I watched him lay in bed with tears in his eyes. I was hit with boldness and anger at that moment. Boldness to say what I was about to say to my elder and anger because I understood if the devil could get into his mind, he could have a field day. I was annoyed by what my uncle said and didn't have time for gentle, loving words of encouragement. I had a word of urgency and correction. Without thinking twice, I blurted out with a stern voice:

"As a minister of the Gospel, you know better than to let those words come out of your mouth. Listen; you know your word better than half the people around you. God has you here for a reason, and if He wanted you dead, He would have taken you long ago. Still, He didn't, so now you can either choose to walk and live on purpose, pray, and do what you need to do in this place, or you can choose to lay here and die. But until then, decide how you plan on living out the rest of your days."

Still in a rage, I stormed out of his room and went home. I guess that put a fire under his butt! Sometimes, we need people to be bold and brave to let us know our stuff is stinking a little.

I returned to visit about a week or two later; I noticed he was up, happy, and smiling. He began going to church every Sunday and attending bible study. He started getting active again. My uncle went back to therapy. And y'all: he was walking again! My Great-Uncle Sidney was now a new man. He got involved with activities and no longer wallowed in misery.

Then, right before his 80th birthday, my great-uncle and I had a conversation. He began to share the following:

"I remember every October: I would go crazy. I didn't understand what it was, but it would trigger something inside me. But this year, I was ready. This October, I saw that black shadow that had been following me around for years. That black shadow tried to take control of me. But I stopped and looked at that shadow for the first time, and I said I know who you are, and I know who I am. Satan, you have no place or authority over me or my mind here. No longer will I allow you to control me. I command you to go in the mighty name of Christ Jesus. I decree and declare that God's blood is over me. I started declaring scriptures over myself, and it fled. It had to flee under the sound of my voice. I've been dealing with depression for all of those years. God healed me at the age of 79!"

I just responded with an "Amen! God healed you from the Black Shadow."

Internally, I thought he had lost his rabbit mind again, and someone forgot to give him his meds or slipped him something. But little did I know what was next. About a week or two after that conversation, I received a phone call from his case worker from the state of Michigan, and she told me:

"Your uncle no longer needs his medication. My evaluation of him has been cleared. He is fine. There's nothing wrong with him."

I couldn't believe my ears. I asked her if she was sure at least three times. When I hung up that phone call, my mouth dropped. My uncle was telling the truth. He was healed from Bipolar Schizophrenia Disorder! My uncle chose to pick up his bed and walk. He stood firm on God's word against the enemy and won!

Let's heal and overcome

Miracles may not happen immediately; sometimes, you must be patient. During a storm, you must keep your faith and envision victory.

Sometimes you will have to wait it out and stay the course. As you trust God, believing it will all work out for His good. Amen! Be encouraged, knowing that to fight this battle; it is important that one arm themselves with the full armor of God, a support group, and in some cases, medication if needed. A majority of people battling with mental issues can be from a spiritual issue. True deliverance can be done, especially if this is something seen generationally.

I also suggest Joyce Meyer's book "The Battlefield of the Mind." I was responsible for my uncle's care for exactly nine years as of 2018. I've learned so much about healthcare, responsibilities, love, and trust; how my dreams are prophetic, and the importance of prayer through the years. (There was a time when I had to go against his wishes. God said it was not his time yet! Although he cussed me out, he thanked me later). I now understand the journey was not a burden at all but a pure blessing and honor.

Pray

Father, in the name of Jesus, I come before You, asking You to show me the root cause of my depression. Father, I ask that You guard my heart, mind, and spirit. Strengthen me, Oh God. Hide Your word in my heart so I can rise above my dark days. Speak Your word over me and make the enemy flee just as You did for Your son, Sidney, that day. He overcame this very thing. Father, Your word says You are my refuge and a stronghold in times of trouble. I am crying out to You, asking that as I rest in You, Your favor will last a lifetime, and depression, bipolar disorder, hallucinations, schizophrenia, and the like, will loose me, my family, and generations after me. That it has no authority in my bloodline. I thank you, Father, for keeping me. Father, I pray the same mind that is in Christ Jesus be in me. Amen.

What's T.R.U?

You or someone you know may have experienced depression, bipolar disorder, or schizophrenia. It looks like there is no hope or healing in sight.

What's Truth?

God's Word says; "Let the wise hear and increase in learning, and the one who understands obtain guidance." (Proverbs 1:5)

"All scripture is breathed out by God and profitable for teaching, for reproof, for correction, and for training in righteousness, that the man of God may be complete, equipped for every good work." (2 Timothy 3:16-17)

"Let this mind be in you, which was also in Christ Jesus." (Philippians 2:5 KJV)

14

No Longer Rejected

Whoever listens to you listens to me; whoever rejects you rejects me; but whoever rejects me rejects him who sent me.
- Luke 10:16

Abuse and Trauma have been known to open the door to rejection. And rejection can open a door leading to unforgiveness. This topic can be expounded upon deeply as its the foundation of many of our wounds, such as fear, pride, double-mindedness, shame, depression, indecision, perversion, and paranoia, just to name a few. For many, rejection started in the womb and may have been passed down through generational DNA. Some experienced this at an older age. Whenever the pain of rejection made an ugly appearance in your life, understand it was strategic to knock you off of your predestined journey. I want to encourage you at this moment as there's healing, love, and acceptance through Christ Jesus. Rejection is one wound which often rears its ugly head around from time to time. I often fight this through prayer at family functions and when I'm face-to-face with one of my known abusers. I'm reminded when my voice isn't heard, when my brown skin offends someone, etc.

Listen, "life is going to life," and rejection will come in many forms, which is why knowing some of the subtle signs is half the battle:

- Not getting a job or the position you felt qualified for;

- Failed relationships or friendships;

- Rejection can surely enter in, for those entering entrepreneurship and ministry;

- Your past can cause others to reject you;

- When a marriage proposal is turned down;

- Being turned down by a crush from childhood or older years;

- Your appearance;

- Not being picked for something you worked very hard for;

- Experiencing a divorce (perspectives as a child or an adult); or

- When a parent holds one child higher than the other.

When we think about the Bible, and history in general, we understand rejection existed long before we were born. Yet, in noticing this tactic being used over and over again by the enemy, we can be more equipped to fight this battle. Stories of man rejecting God, God gives a warning and rejects man, Jesus, the Ultimate Sacrifice is rejected, and man rejects man allowing the cycle to continue. The feelings of rejection can be embarrassing and hurtful, leading many to have self-doubt and depression.

When I was 19, I embarked on a journey to find truth and purpose. I vowed only to date when God gave me a sense of peace. I didn't want any distractions from my seeking God. So for six months, I strictly sought God daily. Praying, studying His word, and surrounding myself with ministers and prayer warriors. During this time, I allowed myself to be vulnerable with God. His love was so unconditional I no longer felt rejected. My biggest teacher was a friend of the family, Marvin, an ordained minister. He taught me how to listen to the Bible on a CD or via DVD. He gave me no excuses when it came to learning my word.

He introduced me to prayer warriors when I had no clue what a prayer warrior was. I didn't understand why they were speaking in a language that sounded similar to what some may call gibberish. I was shocked to hear they got together on certain days every week to pray and fast for others outside of Lent. However, something deep down inside my heart felt what I was witnessing was the power of God moving through them. They each loved on me so much that I cried all the time. How can people know your sins and love you harder? I couldn't answer that then, but I knew it had to be God.

One day I decided to give praying from deep in my heart with moaning and groaning a shot. As I started to seek the Lord more and more, I found more of Him. This was around the time my grandmother had gotten really sick. During her transition, my friend, now single, was again the only male friend there for my family and me. He stayed with us the whole time of her transition and after. He even supported my family in a few ways, helping with my grieving and the funeral. It was at that moment I began to look at him differently. He went from a "friend zone" to God, showing me visions of his true identity. A strong, honorable, respectful man who would make someone a very happy wife one day. A family member once told me: "You should keep him as a friend because he is a good guy, and You may mess it up." I truly believed those words and tried to push him away daily, but he loved me even more, just like God, Marvin, and those prayer warriors.

I spoke to my father via an email confessing the powerful impact of his departure during my childhood and its effects on issues hindering me from wanting to be married. I felt if he had stayed closer, so many things would never have happened. I wondered if I would get a divorce like my parents, and I wasn't even married yet! I wondered if I would be a good wife. I wondered if I was ready for this. Am I too damaged for this man? I wondered if he would reject me like many others once I fully opened up.

God had to remind me of who I was. He said, "I wasn't my parents. I am my own person and can only fail if I give up!"

My friend would always say when he gets married, divorce is not an option in the sense of not making it the first choice every time tough moments presented themselves. Yet, in the back of my mind, I felt divorce was an option because I saw my parents choose it for themselves. I shared with him that I might not be able to have children, and he accepted me. I told him all of my deepest darkest secrets, and he loved me even more. He prayed with and for me. "Who is this man?" I thought! He had to be too good to be true. I often wondered if he was crazy or if God gave him the patience and strength to deal with me.

My friend proposed, and during pre-marital counseling, I learned all the stuff that was building up inside me for so many years. It was too much for me to dump on and expect my future husband to fix. It wasn't his job. He didn't hurt me or do any of those things to me. His job was to be my support and to love me. It took us some time to find our groove, but we did. And in 2008, we became Mr. & Mrs. Brian Williams. On our wedding day, though I felt scared, I also felt happy, excited, and nervous all in one. I knew if I was going to give this thing a shot, it would be with him for sure.

I never envisioned myself being married until one night after our wedding: God brought back to my memory a dream I had about a year and a half prior.

In this dream, I was getting married at my childhood church. I wore a beautiful ivory and bronze wedding dress, and my soon-to-be husband wore an all-ivory tuxedo. We were standing on a cloud and exchanging our vows; I knew he was a lighter-skin African-American male. I couldn't see his face. All I could see was the back of his head; he was taller than me. When I looked at our wedding photos, tears began to fall down my face. One photo stood out from all the others. This photo showed the back of our clothes. It was at that very moment I knew Brian was the man in my dream. He was literally the man who God showed me I would marry.

Listen, I am so full of happiness when I think about how intentional God truly is. He put me together with a man who is very gentle and patient with me. I am forever grateful for that, and I thank God for our Union. No, he isn't perfect, but he is who I needed to do life with on this earth. I thank God for our covenant. It wasn't my lifestyle. I didn't always live a life reflecting Christ. A straight sinner I was. Some couldn't understand why God allowed me to get married to such an amazing man.

I never idolized marriage. I didn't know I needed Brian, and he didn't know he needed me until we said, "I do." My heart only wanted to crave, seek, and search for God. I wanted to know Him. I wanted to know why I was dealt the hand I was dealt. I wanted answers only He could give me. In return, He blessed me with a help-mate I could grow with, someone who would love me, and I could love him, a partner in Christ. God blessed me with someone who could lead our family and me as the priest of our home. Although we work individually and have our missions, we still work together. Our marriage journey is a gift from God because I finally decided to seek God. Thanks to Marvin and his crew of prayer warriors.

Through my marriage, Brian introduced me to the people who later became my spiritual parents and wise counsel. They eventually ordained me to teach about Christ and to know Christ Jesus personally. They taught me all they knew so I could be transformed, healed, delivered, and free to help someone else.

Let's heal and overcome

We must identify where our rejection began as we continue our healing journey. In other words, "Ask God to show you the root cause of your rejection." As faith followers, we must remember that Jesus was despised and rejected. Therefore, our lives are not exempt. However, not everyone around me was negative. I was surrounded by some loving family and friends; nothing replaced the type of love I was looking for in my parents.

It was as if I was always wanting their attention, and their responses were the only ones that mattered.

As life went on, I opened my heart to let God fill those wounds. I learned the importance of arming ourselves daily with the full armor of God from Ephesians 6:10-20 and the effectiveness of daily prayer, not only for ourselves but for our family, friends, loved ones, and communities. It truly takes patience, strength, self-reflection, prayer, worship, and crying out to God to fix some things, but it starts with us. Be encouraged, knowing He will restore those things which were lost, and you can overcome anything with Christ Jesus!

God began my healing journey from rejection first through HIS love, then through the love of many others who welcomed my broken self with open arms. God brought restoration to my relationship with my dad, and I no longer hold my parents accountable for what I've allowed to keep me in bondage and pain.

Pray

Father, today I humbly come before You asking that You forgive me for hiding rejection in my heart for myself and others. Father, I ask that You search my heart and be merciful if I've ever rejected others. Have mercy on my family, friends, co-workers, peers, and any other persons who have rejected me. Father, I thank You that Your perfect love casts out fear, including the fear of rejection. Father, today, I decree and declare that I am free from the wound of rejection. I will no longer take rejection personally. Nor will I walk in pride, self-pity, or bitterness. Father, Jeremiah 29:11 says: "For I know the plans I have for you, declares the Lord, plans for welfare and not for evil, to give you a future and a hope." So today, I'm choosing to stand on hope. Hope that the feeling of rejection will no longer consume me. People rejected Your Son, Christ Jesus, who was perfect. So Father, heal me, my heart and mind. Thank You for loving me and not rejecting me through my days here on earth. In Jesus' name, I pray. Amen.

What's T.R.U.?

Rejection was once your story. It caused you much pain. Isolation is where the enemy wants you. Creating a wound so deep it made space for things you've never imagined. This wound was masked with layers on layers. For some, the rejection from others led to the rejection of self and, ultimately, the rejection of God, which created a chosen lifestyle living outside His presence.

What's Truth?

God wants to restore you and let you know you're no longer a victim of rejection, and His Word says: "As you come to him, the living Stone—rejected by humans but chosen by God and precious to him." (1 Peter 2:4 NIV)

"But he said to me, 'My grace is sufficient for you, for my power is made perfect in weakness.' Therefore I will boast all the more gladly about my weaknesses, so that Christ's power may rest on me." (2 Corinthians 12:9 NIV)

"For you created my inmost being; you knit me together in my mother's womb. I praise you because I am fearfully and wonderfully made; your works are wonderful, I know that full well." (Psalm 139:13-14 NIV)

15

A Second Chance

Almost losing one person you love shines a bright spotlight on life and suddenly strips you of everything but your real feelings. – Fannie Flagg

I CAN'T TELL YOU how long my son and I were unconscious. However, I can recall being awakened by a room full of doctors! While wearing an oxygen mask, a steady rhythm of chest compressions was being performed on me. Doctors and nurses were screaming, "We have the mom's heartbeat. Let's prep her for an emergency cesarean. Stay with us, Mom. We thought we had lost you. Stay calm. We are still working on the baby."

With tears rolling down my face, I could barely get the following words out,

"Is he going to be, OK? Is my son, OK??"

One of the doctors replied:

"We are working on it, but you must keep your oxygen mask on!"

I internally cried out to God,

"God, YOU said that I would have a son. YOU said to name him Joshua. You said you forgave me, Lord. I don't want to lose this one. You said the blood of Jesus covers us. SAVE HIM, PLEASE..."

Words, like a whisper, came out of my mouth. I prayed:

"Our Father, which art in heaven, hallow be thy name, thy kingdom come, thy will be done, on earth as it is in heaven, give us this..."

Beep, Beep, Beep...

"We have a heartbeat for baby!"

I had never been more excited about a hospital monitor sound in my life. Smiles, joy, and praises filled the room that day. It was as if we all knowingly understood the miracle that took place.

"God is for us the God of our deliverance. The Lord GOD rescues us from death." - Psalm 68:20 ISV

———◦◦◦———

I'm not sure why, but for years the enemy had been trying to interfere with the birth of Joshua. From the near performance of an emergency hysterectomy to the reminders of my past. From the diagnosis of pre-cancerous cells on my cervix to speaking infertility over me.

"But GOD!"

God's word was firm and true. Although my son and I died briefly in May of 2010, God saved us, made us both new, and I'm forever grateful. He breathed life over us so we could do His will on earth. We are both still here for a reason, and Joshua's purpose/mission in life is so great even I pray God keeps and protects him.

Fear, amongst other things, will not be his nor your portion. I'm not sure if our children will ever understand what we as parents go through for them, but one thing for sure is Joshua will know God spared him, which means his life is greater than he knows!

On this journey, I want you all to evaluate when you encountered something in your life which may not have been an issue of infertility but of constant attacks on your health, finances, or faith, which caused you to question God about why this keeps happening. What part of your life do you need to die to? I want you to understand God is working in the background, and although arrows may form in your life, they will not prosper. I'm here to bear witness to you. Each of you, your child(ren), rather natural, adopted, or spiritual, have a purpose. Your life is a miracle, and the blood of Jesus is covering you and your family even when you can't see it.

The healing process

Fear can be a debilitating emotion that can keep us from achieving our goals and living life to the fullest. But fear doesn't have to consume us. We can learn how to overcome the wounds from unhealthy fear and embrace a healthy awe of God. With a proper understanding of what fear is, we can recognize it for what it is and learn how to move past it. By learning how to practice self-care, develop healthy coping mechanisms, and build up our faith in God, we can begin the journey of overcoming fear and finding peace in our lives. Faith as small as a mustard seed and a willing heart is all God needs from each of us. Thus, acknowledging and facing our fears can help us realize most of the time, our imagination was far worse than the actual task or event. Fear can sometimes cause us to think irrationally. Fear itself, as a fickle emotion, wasn't created to harm us. It was placed so we would have a built-in fight or flight mode. Yet, it can be both healthy and unhealthy. When we give unhealthy fear power, it can lead to wounds that prevent us from living our fullest potential, passing up opportunities, and causing relationship issues.

On the other hand, embracing a healthy awe of God and His promises can help us overcome these wounds and live with courage, confidence, and hope. Second chances are never easy, but they can be rewarding if we choose to take them. God gives us grace and mercy, which allows us many chances. It is important to remember that no matter what happened in the past, we can choose to make our lives better today. With strength and courage, it is possible to find new paths and opportunities for growth even after experiencing difficult times, facing fears, and embracing faith over fear.

Prayer

Lord, I thank You that my battles are already won. I trust You with my life and my family's lives, and as I come before Your throne, I thank You for showing me the way through Your Son, Holy Spirit, and Word. Lord, just as You knew me before I was sent here on this earth, I pray that You continue to cover me with Your blood. Direct my path and heart and keep my children and me from premature death. Open my spiritual eyes to see what You have for me; Lord, equip me with what I need this season. Lord, show me what my soul and flesh need to die too. Lord, forgive me for my sins, known and unknown. Lord, heal me from all things wicked and not like You. Lord, increase my faith. Father, I thank You in advance, and most importantly, I thank You for Your constant love even when I don't deserve it! Amen.

What's T.R.U.?

You may have experienced infertility and constant attacks in many life areas. You may feel hopeless at this very moment. You may feel you have no more chances.

What's Truth?

God's Word says: "Therefore if anyone is in Christ, he is a new creation. The old has passed away; behold, the new has come." (2 Corinthians 5:17)

"For I know the plans I have for you, declares the Lord, plans for welfare and not for evil, to give you a future and a hope."(Jeremiah 29:11)

"May the God of hope fill you with all joy and peace in believing, so that by the power of the Holy Spirit you may abound in hope." (Romans 15:13)

16

No Condemnation

*For God did not send his Son into the world to condemn
the world, but in order that the world might be saved
through him. – John 3:17*

HAVE YOU EVER FELT condemned about something in your life? Do
you know that feeling of disapproval, punishment, or sentencing? [20]
I sure have many times. But that is not of God. He gives us correction
and love. Please know we will have a consequence for our actions,
but once he says we are free, we are free indeed. Now this is not an
invitation to repeat our offenses again and again. It is, however, a
time of reflection, to look inwardly, to see if the condemnation you
feel is because you aren't truly healed. A good quote by Harper Lee
says, "A man can condemn his enemies, but knowing them is wiser."
I believe we can sometimes be our own enemy because we have yet to
know who we truly are. If we did, condemnation wouldn't be how
we respond immediately to ourselves or others. We would respond
with love, correction, and wisdom.

In my bedroom, I began to cry out to God. I prayed with my whole heart,
body, mind, soul, and spirit. With everything inside of me, I asked God,
"Why me?" Why did he choose me to be a mother? I have sinned and
didn't deserve this title. As tears dropped from my eyes profusely, I asked
God to forgive me for those abortions and to free me from my thoughts

and actions. I asked him to keep my unborn child and me throughout this pregnancy.

You know what?

He forgave me right then and there. He answered me and said:

"You are already forgiven."

Everything I laid before God had been erased when I repented that night. The enemy tried to make me feel more horrible, reminding me of the choices I wasn't proud of. Unfortunately, I played a massive part by standing in agreement with him. Nevertheless, this time, I did not abort my mission or position. The Lord told me all was well, and He loves me. He told me not to worry; His Yes means Yes, and His No means No. It's forgiven. He is not a man that He should lie. He is the God Almighty. He is the same God that forgave even the wicked.

So what makes what I've done different? He is the same God who turned a man named Saul, who once crucified Christians, into Paul, who helped build the church as we know it today. God said, "I showed favor upon the lady at the well and so many more. My word hasn't changed; I haven't changed. I still love you with unconditional love as you've never known. So now, allow me to be Who and What you need."

He then showed me a vision of a man who would be my son one day. That brought me to even more tears. I had to step out on faith and take the first step by repenting and asking for forgiveness. I could be freed, forgiven, healed, and delivered by His grace and power. My heart wanted to change, so my actions had to follow suit!

Let's heal and overcome

If you have ever experienced an abortion or aborted something you started? For whatever reason; I know how heavy that can be. The condemnation you put on yourself is far worse than anyone else can say about you! But I want you to know something: God is forgiving. So, sis, forgive yourself. You are not a murderer. But owning that, the roles of instigator or accomplice you played a huge part in and surrendering that to God. Forgive others involved as well. David wasn't perfect by any means, but he made a covenant with God never to take his spirit away from him and to keep his family for generations. Even he prayed, "Feel my pain and see my trouble. Forgive all my sins."

> Hebrews 8:12 says: "And I will forgive their wickedness, and I will never again remember their sins."

Know once it's forgiven, God erases it from your book. The trick of the enemy continues to tell you God is mad at you, you should still be ashamed because of your sin, and God can't use you (fill in the blank____). Sister, you have to arm yourself with the whole armor of God! Hold up that shield of faith to stop the fiery arrows of the devil.

You may have had tons of false starting businesses, writing a book, finishing school, etc., and it's constantly eating at you. Remember, you don't have to live with this wound. God's word says, "Don't let evil conquer you but conquer evil by doing good."[21] You have to know when we hurt, God hurts.

The mental, emotional, and spiritual self-torment can last for years. We begin to heal from the aftermath by acknowledging the wound, being honest before the Father, and repenting. Yet once you pray and your heart is serious, God will heal you. You may have to continue speaking positive, Bible-based affirmations daily, as each day presents challenges.

Therefore, by choosing to speak life, we can conquer the negative thoughts trying to creep back into one's mind; one must resist them. Put God's word on it and tell Satan, "You have no place here! I command you to go in the name of Jesus!" Do not come into agreement with the negativity.

I'm not encouraging abortions; let's get that straight. I'm clearly stating; if you have already done the act and are not healed and delivered from it, God wants you to know you no longer have to live in bondage or suffer in silence. Statistics say: One in three women will have an abortion in her lifetime. This is a vast number of women, and I, for one, could not go a day longer without sharing my story with the hopes of helping someone heal or thinking twice about deciding to do something of this magnitude.

Sis, God wants to use you to turn things around for His good. He loves you unconditionally. Be encouraged and stand firm on God's word! Life tends to give us choices. With every choice, there is either a negative or positive outcome! But Christ can turn your negative into a positive for His Glory!

Pray

Father, my heart is crying out to You. I want to receive the healing You have for me. I want to trust Your word that You died for all my sins. Father, I repent for aborting my babies, aborting my mission, having a lustful spirit, taking morning-after pills, and coming into agreement with the enemy and the enemy within myself. I am not my past. Father, help me fight for peace of mind, healing, deliverance, and legacy. Heal me from the spirit of murder, fear, unforgiveness, guilt, and shame. Father, I repent for every generation that aborted before me. And Father, I pray that this spirit will not touch the generations after me. I bind the spirit of abortion. In the name of Jesus, I thank you. Amen.

What's T.R.U.?

Yes, the enemy tried to condemn you and indeed tried to keep you bound, but God said, "No!"

What's Truth?

God's Word says: "And the free gift is not like the result of that one man's sin. For the judgment following one trespass brought condemnation, but the free gift following many trespasses brought justification." (Romans 5:16)

"Whoever believes in him is not condemned, but whoever does not believe is condemned already, because he has not believed in the name of the only Son of God." (John 3:18)

"If we confess our sins, he is faithful and just to forgive us our sins and to cleanse us from all unrighteousness." (1 John 1:9)

17

Freedom From Addiction

Though no one can go back and make a brand-new start,
anyone can start from now and make a brand-new ending.
– Carl Bard

MANY OF US COPE with our traumas in many ways. I've found drugs and alcohol to be the quick fix for many women and men. The pain of our past can be so heavy and, honestly, too much to endure sober-minded, especially when you feel like an island of your own.

As a child, I could never come to grips with why so many of my beautiful family members no longer looked like the beautiful men and women they were in those picture books. It was as if they were frozen in time through family photo albums. They became new people. Hard to look at on the outside and rough to deal with on the inside. I would overhear family talking and whispering, and yet those same voices became silent, and no one wanted to address the elephant in the room. I'm sure you have heard of families where drug and alcohol addiction was no stranger. It was like a written code where we didn't interact with them as we would with the other members of the family.

All of us children knew to lock up our personal belongings such as cash, jewelry, and anything worth something. Or, on some occasions, we would hide the good alcohol in another room or in weird containers. Yet, within the same scene, I watched some hiding in dark places, sneaking and enabling those same family members they just warned us, kids, about. This made absolutely no sense to me. As much as it hurt my young heart to see loved ones deal with addictions, it hurt me all the more knowing this could become my story.

By the 5th grade, I was drinking to keep my mind off the constant abuse I was dealing with. and once 7th grade rolled around, I was introduced to marijuana and cigars. Those became my substances of choice; without them, I felt like I couldn't make it through the day.

Just a little weed

In middle school, I was offered every drug you could imagine for a child growing up in the 90s, but the thought of looking like or being treated like my family members with addictions stayed in the back of my mind. I guess my hint of vainness helped because I loved my appearance so much; there was no way I was going to let myself go out like that. So, I smoked a little weed and drank alcohol. The people around me partied hard and often. We, kids, had free range to do just about anything. It also meant just about anything could be done to us as well.

Going into my senior year of high school, I vowed to stop smoking marijuana. During this one particular night, I was the only one who knew how to roll the weed correctly. At first, I refused since I no longer smoked. I told them they needed to learn how to help their own habits. But there I was; after enough peer pressure; rolling the blunt for them and walking away while they smoked. As I went to get something to eat, I ran into one of my friends from school. He had become a police officer and scorned me about rolling that stuff for my friends. Even though I was not smoking, I was still enabling them. I told him that I wouldn't do it again, and I really meant it.

Heading home that night, two ladies were driving down the same street as us, speeding with no lights on. They crashed into our car, sending us into someone's front porch, just barely missing their living room. That night I was the one who bore the brunt of the accident. I was sitting in the back seat but left the scene in an ambulance feeling the weight of the conversation I just had with my old schoolmate. Thinking to myself, "Man, if I never rolled that weed for them, none of us would've been in this accident."

How it ended

I tried smoking weed three times after that, but it didn't work out for me. My own cousin tried to lace my weed with some harder drugs. I trusted no one after that. Years later, while sitting in my car talking to a friend, I was smoking a mild cigar, and out of nowhere, I had a seizure. After that night, I stopped smoking for good. This is only a small part of my story. I could go on and on, and I know you could as well.

God showed Himself throughout my life, keeping me, my mind, my body, and my soul. What I didn't share with many people was that I carried a little green pocket bible with me everywhere I went. I would read while I was smoking, wondering if the pages in that book really had substance, were the words real, and could these prayers work during my generation.

Have you ever looked in the mirror and seen yourself as a different person? I did. Internally, I was crying out to Jesus, asking Him to take away the addiction and desire to smoke from me. These were personal moments I was seeking in private. You may feel marijuana is not that bad, but when it's used for non-medical reasons, it can cause more harm than good. You may not have dealt with marijuana addiction but mushrooms, pills (street & prescription), crack, cocaine, heroin, and the like. You may have thought of God not being real or feelings of being so far gone that Jesus wouldn't even want to use you. Maybe you feel you've used drugs for so long that you can't survive if you stop.

Listen, I'm here to tell you that your wound is deeper than drugs. Yet, God wants you to give it all to Him. He still wants to use you and heal your brokenness and unbelief. He wants to free you from your addictions. But you have to want it; you have to give Him permission to heal you. That's how free will works. That seizure I experienced was an unfortunate circumstance from the outside looking in, but to me, it was an answered prayer, and I thanked Jesus for hearing my voice and healing me, a sinner.

Drinks anyone?

Casual drinking was never just casual for me. What starts off as a taste; grows into shots, cups, then bottles. Have you ever asked yourself, "Why am I doing this?" While out partying and having a great time? If we are being honest, probably not! This section is not for those of you who have never had a drink in your life but for the ones who are still dealing with the wounds of life. Have you noticed a pattern of needing a drink when one of the following occurs:

- Death of a loved one

- Traumatic memory

- Financial issues

- Divorce, Breakup

- Need to feel in control or brave

- To have fun

- Escaping your truth and reality

- Peer Pressure

- Health Issues

- Fill   in   the
  blank:_____

Drinking to deal with our life issues or past traumas only creates new problems. In college, I can recall having drinks with my friend, who was a pharmacy major. We were talking about our problems. Next thing you know, he took out some prescribed pills, crunched them up, and began to sniff them! My eyes opened so wide, and I sobered up real quick. He told me this is how he deals with his problems and suggested I try it. I declined, but he continued. Once the pills kicked in, he started panicking and took off running up and down our dorm halls. I decided that day that no matter what, I would stick to alcohol, and I did.

I drank every day. Just as I judged that young man and his classmates openly, I was no different behind closed doors. I couldn't go one day without taking at least one shot of liquor. This was a secret I held on to for years, masking my alcohol with scented lotions and breath mints. The pain of facing my reality was getting to be too much for me. Past traumas, new traumas, and life were overwhelming. Many times, trying to stop, I failed over and over again.

I came into contact with a family friend one day, and as we stood in the kitchen, he told me I was too beautiful just to let myself go like many others before me. He said God had bigger plans for me, and my beauty was not for me but for God. He told me to take care of my temple. I took those words to heart, and I held on to them. I didn't understand all of what he meant at the time, but I knew it was something serious.

Struggling with any addiction can be tough; I get it, but the more we rely on drugs or alcohol to help mask our deepest wounds, pains, and traumas, we are doing ourselves a disservice with these quick fixes, which create other issues. God wants us healed. He wants our honesty, our hearts, and our YES. God wants to take your pain and bring it purpose. Listen, I understand that this book may not drive you to heal completely or stop causing yourself more wounds. But it may help plant those seeds that you just might hold on to as you move about your journey.

How it ended

After a long night of drinking, I woke up with the worst hangover. I'm sure I ate a million ginger candies and drank all the Gatorade in the store.

Yet I couldn't move. My son asked me what was wrong, and I lied! Yep, I lied like a cheap rug. I told him I was sick.

That encounter with my son made me think to myself, and I didn't want him to see me again in a drunken state. I didn't want to lie to him anymore. I wanted to be better as a mother, and thoughts of my childhood flashed before my eyes.

See, it wasn't just about me anymore; I had a child. I came from a family that suffered from addiction and mental health issues. Somebody had to overcome and break those family curses and heal the wounds of alcohol addiction.

God took the taste right out of my mouth completely 4 years later. Now I get nauseous and headaches from the smell of alcohol. This one took a little longer than the smoking, but I prayed without ceasing for myself. I spoke it, and I envisioned myself healed. I believed God would do it by faith, and once my heart actually wanted what my words were saying BAM! Like that, it happened. I got deliverance and healing through yet another private prayer!

The healing process

To begin the healing process from the wounds of alcohol and drug addiction, we have first to admit there is a problem. The Bible talks about those that have done drugs via hallucinogenics; it talks about many drunks as well. Noah was found drunk and naked,[22] and Lot's story[23] is disturbing. His daughters got him drunk so they could have children. Talk about incest and date rape before it was a thing!

Rather you are struggling with alcohol or drugs, they will have you involved in moments you hoped were all a dream. God still used Noah and Lot just like He will use you. Having a drink of wine is not a sin; it's not bad at all. When it becomes an idol in our lives, when we start to turn to those things before God, we open our lives to addiction.

I understand that, with many things in life, it all takes time, strength, and power only God can give us. I can be honest in saying I had to learn how to say NO; I had to surround myself with people who were strong enough to help me when I felt weak. I tested the Word of God for myself. Whenever I felt an urge to drink because I didn't want to deal with something or felt stressed out and overwhelmed, I would open my Bible, talk to God, and read topics that I was struggling with that day. I called my spiritual mother to pray with and for me. I called on others in the faith until I was strong enough to stand on my own.

Let's heal and overcome

Not all addictions can be treated equally. Each person has to truly look within and find where this addiction started. What is keeping you in this place? Do you even want to heal from this wound? These are questions we need to reflect on as we move along. It's easy for us to make excuses, but if our hearts are not truly ready, then the cycle will continue to repeat itself over and over again. If you are not ready or want to heal from addiction, then by all means, stop right here.

But for those that want to move forward, below are a few tips to help get you started, and I have included some resources in the back of this book for you as well.

- Having a safe place or person to talk to is very important.

- Know your triggers. You may have to remove yourself from certain people, places, and things.

- Stop and ask yourself, why am I drinking or taking this drug? If it's connected to current emotions, depression, trauma, and the like, stop and reflect on how you can attack this situation differently. I found that exercising, deep breathing, going to the water, dancing, and doing things to take my mind away helped until my initial urge to indulge went away.

- Repent, and ask God to give you the strength to overcome addiction. Give yourself grace because this takes time; start with minutes, hours, days, months, and years.

- Depending on the severity, you may need to check into a center, join groups or find a church with programs that can help you along your journey.

———————◆———————

Pray

Father, today I come before You asking that You heal me from the wounds of alcohol and/or drug addiction. Father, I know this road is not easy, but I know You will be with me along the journey. Take the desires and taste from my mouth. Father show me how to face life sober-minded. Give me strength on the days I may feel weak. Father, direct my steps to the right people and places. Remove me from those that are no good for me. Father, Your Word says in Ephesians 5:18 do not get drunk on wine, which leads to debauchery. Instead, be filled with the Spirit. So, Father, I ask that You fill me with Your spirit and cleanse me from the inside out. Help me to stay sober-minded and alert; in the name of Jesus, I pray, Amen.

What's T.R.U?

Yes, it's T.R.U. that you may have experienced alcohol and/or drug addiction. You may feel as if there is no hope and fear in facing life sober-minded. You may be in denial that you have an addiction.

What's What's Truth?

God's Word says; "Be alert and sober-minded. Your enemy, the devil, prowls around like a roaring lion looking for someone to devour." (1 Peter 5:8)

"Wine is a mocker and beer a brawler; whoever is led astray by them is not wise." (Proverbs 20:1 NIV)

"Above all else, guard your heart, for everything you do flows from it." (Proverbs 4:23 NIV)

18

From The Wall to The People

Have I not commanded you? Be strong and courageous.
Do not be afraid; do not be discouraged, for the LORD
your God will be with you wherever you go. - Joshua 1:9
(NIV)

I DIDN'T LIKE MY voice; I didn't feel heard or competent. I also didn't truly love myself. I had an unshakable fear that caused issues in every area of my life, and I could not stop giving fear a voice. It took many years before I had grown to understand that public speaking can be a daunting task for many of us. The fear of speaking in front of a crowd can be overwhelming and paralyzing. But it doesn't have to be that way. With the right approach, we can learn to overcome our fear and become confident speakers. God had called me to ministry, and the enemy attacked my voice as a child to derail the plans God had for my life.

No longer muzzled

The first step to start moving past fear is to let go of our anxieties and embrace the healing power of Jesus, and love ourselves the way God made us. Once we start to accept ourselves, we can start working on our confidence and begin the journey toward becoming an effective speaker. We can take small steps, such as joining a Toastmasters club or attending public speaking classes, which will help us build up our skills over time—maybe starting a podcast or recording personal videos that we keep until we are led to share them. By taking these steps, we can eventually overcome our fear of public speaking and use it as an opportunity to express ourselves confidently in front of one person, a small group, or an audience.

Fear from trauma

I didn't overcome fear overnight. I was clueless about the first step. It just so happened I was watching Joyce Meyer one day, and she preached a message on "Facing Fear Courageously." By doing things afraid. That day, I made a conscious decision to no longer allow fear to control my life. I began to do things courageously, even if my initial emotion was fear, and I would do it one day at a time. As time passed, I noticed there were still some fears I could not shake.

While in prayer, I asked God to bring things to my memory and show me the root cause of this toxic fear issue. I saw a vision of those old houses I would walk past as a child. I saw faces and smelled scents that once triggered me. Then it hit me. I had a deep fear of men, a fear of what-ifs, and a fear of speaking. My fear was rooted deep in my trauma. I encourage you to take the time right now to ask God to show you where the wound of fear was planted in your life.

For many of us, our fear stems from our youth. During our younger years, we have yet to know our whole identity and who and whose we indeed are in Christ Jesus. We are so vulnerable. We believe every word from incredibly sneaky, conniving, perverted teens, adults, and others. By acknowledging this big elephant in the room trying to hinder many of us, God will give us freedom and tools. I searched "fear not" in my Bible app and stopped counting after 123. This means we have over 123 weapons to use toward that wound. Some sources say the Bible contains 365 verses, and others mention it's over 400; either way, that lets us know that an unhealthy fear is one of satan's oldest tricks in the book. See, satan isn't original; he is a duplicator and will take what God meant for good and turn it into something evil or perverted. According to research, there are hundreds of phobias connected to fear.[24] But God never intended for us to fear in those capacities. Proverbs 19:23 (AMPC) says: "The revenant, worshipful fear of the Lord leads to life, and he who has it rests satisfied; he cannot be visited with (actual) evil."

Joyce Meyer says it best in her book, Living Courageously: You Can Face Anything, Just Do It Afraid: "The fear of the Lord is the beginning of all proper knowledge and wisdom." Our relationship with God will give us knowledge and understanding of correct or wrong fear. Psalm 34:7 says, "The angel of the Lord encamps around those who fear him (who revere and worship Him with awe), and each of them He delivers. Let's take a second to define reverential; it simply states: *"The adjective reverential comes close to implying worship — a devoutly religious person feels reverential toward God, for example. It's rooted in the Latin word reverentia, "awe or respect," from revereri, "to stand in awe of, fear, or be afraid of."* [25] Here we learn that the fear of God is a form of worship, respect, to stand in awe!

My God that doesn't sound scary or bad at all. I would compare this to those of us raised by loving parents who were strict for our protection. We wouldn't want to be disrespectful or do something which would be dishonoring. Well, at least not intentionally. This is because of the honor we have for them. We may mess up from time to time, but we wouldn't repeat the offense over and over again. This is the same for God. We fear Him with respect, worship, honor, and submission. It's normal to have a fear of caution or uneasiness. Many people throughout the Bible had that type of fear, but God's word gives us over 365 verses to help us speak to those things. Colossians 3:2 mentions, "The word of God teaches us that we are to set our minds and keep them set on things above, not on things of the earth."

My truth

Writing this book was terrifying, and the spirit of procrastination sat right next to fear. I worried people wouldn't want to buy my book. Why would people want to hear what I had to say? With so many books covering the same topics, what would make me think mine was worth reading? Those were legit questions.

But God impressed on a sister in Christ whom I had never met before. She suggested I check out a link she received from a friend. She told me it might help in my writing. As I clicked the link, I saw the page had a flyer inviting people to join a 7-day writing challenge. This challenge claimed you could finish a book with the right tools, patience, and God! I thought to myself, how crazy is that? It had to be some sales gimmick, but God knew what He was doing.

When I tell you, this was a setup from the beginning. He put me around a group of people with a finisher's spirit: prayer warriors, scribe anointers, natural encouragers, entrepreneurs, and many more. These people had a purpose and wanted others to walk in theirs fully. I joined the challenge and would have my daily bread with the Lord daily. He would take me through healing and deliverance daily as I wrote, and guess what? I began writing this book afraid. Still, I did it with God, prayer, worship, and accountability partners. I wrote it sleepy and wanted to give up, but everyone was encouraging. I couldn't stop! I had to finish and had to grow in many ways!

I became fearless as I wrote, and I could see my children in the first four days of the challenge come to life, step out on faith, and face fears. My heart couldn't have been happier. This all happened because I stepped out on faith and decided fear had no place in my life. As the Dutch Christian author and Holocaust survivor Corrie ten Boom once said: "Never be afraid to trust an unknown future to a known God." I prayed, read my word, worshiped, and meditated on it. When I watched those videos in the writing group, they would fill my cup for the day. They would speak life into all of us, bring about confirmation, and become the "Midwives" in the spirit, as many of us birthed our books!

Let's heal and overcome

Are you dealing with fear? Now is the time God wants for you to get rid of it for good! He wants you to be free so you can be in a position to walk fully in obedience, joy, and courage. Joshua was a great warrior, minister, and man of God. He gained experience from some great men and was a minister to Moses, but even Joshua faced days where he feared. Whenever his spirit began to let fear in, God would tell him:

"Have I not commanded you? Be strong and courageous. Do not be afraid; do not be discouraged, for the Lord your God will be with you wherever you go." - Joshua 1:9

God said do NOT be afraid because He will be with us wherever we go! How awesome is that? He didn't say a few places. He said wherever you go. Fear wants to hold you back and keep you stuck, never reaching your full potential.

Pray

I decree and declare that today unhealthy fear has no place in my life. I say death and curses be removed from myself and my family right now in the name of Jesus. I decree that I will rise and be who God has called me to be; I pray that the spirit of fear, doubt, regret, and confusion be removed from my bloodline. These hindrances have no place in my life anymore! I am a Warrior. God did not give me the spirit of fear but of love, power, and a sound mind. I will rise, overcome the enemy's tricks, and surround myself with other warriors in Christ who pour and speak life over me. I will go back and help someone else get through this fight. I choose to face fear today, knowing I have the power and authority this time. God is with me wherever I go, and I will walk in a healthy fear of God as I reverence Him! - Amen.

What's T.R.U.?

Unhealthy fear has tried to block you and blind you from the healthy fear of God. You are afraid of the unknown.

What's Truth?

God's Word says: "Therefore, since we are receiving a kingdom which cannot be shaken, let us have grace, by which we may serve God acceptably with reverence and Godly fear. For our God is a consuming fire." (Hebrews 12:28-29 NKJV)

"Don't envy sinners, but always continue to fear the LORD. You will be rewarded for this; your hope will not be disappointed." (Proverbs 23:17-18 NLT)

"Fear not, for I am with you; be not dismayed, for I am your God; I will strengthen you. I will help you. I will uphold you with my righteous right hand." (Isaiah 41:10)

19

My Mind Is No Longer a Battlefield

My dark days made me strong. Or maybe I was already strong, and they made me prove it. - Emery Lord

THIS HAS BEEN A known tactic in every part of history. Several accounts of people were recorded who dealt with anxiety throughout scripture. Let's take the story of Moses. He truly carried a heavy load. God came and commanded him to speak to the children of Israel and lead them out of bondage from Egypt. Moses felt incompetent and thought God had chosen the wrong man for the job. Although Moses was filled with many anxieties, God still used him. Moses cried out in hopelessness and despair when things went wrong along this journey. He struggled with anger and extreme fear of men and their faces. He feared Pharoah, his people, public speaking, and so on because he thought his stutter would hinder his being used by God. This brought about much anxiety and many excuses during his life.[26]

As we think about Moses, we can reflect on our own lives. How often have we counted ourselves out by making excuses and talking ourselves into a panic? Yet, a simple research can always present us with someone who's had it worse than us and still managed not to allow adversity, anxiety, or panic to hold them back or limit themselves. I once heard the following saying: "When you think too far into the future, one can bring about anxiety." This tends to be true in many cases.

One night while in the shower, I prayed and asked God to reveal where my anxiety and panic originated. Immediately, memories started to flood my brain like scenes from a movie. Visions of me walking from school as a young girl. Quick flashbacks of seeing older guys outside. Feelings of a paralyzing fear came over me. Terrifying thoughts would run through my mind nonstop: What if they snatched me up and killed me? What if they rape me? How would I escape? Who would help me? What if they torture me? I could feel my younger self having panic attacks, leading to asthma attacks. Memories of running home or walking five blocks in a different direction to avoid seeing the young men felt like I was right there again.

Crazy right?

But at that moment, it was as if a light bulb had gone off. My anxiety was rooted in fear due to the years of trauma I experienced. In that prayer, I was reminded how I suppressed so much of my past. I'd forgotten those intense moments of my youth and moved on unhealed. Nevertheless, you and I, like Moses and others throughout the Bible, are able to recover and move on in life, taking each day as it comes and living a life no longer in darkness and bondage but one of light, freedom, and peace.

The healing process

Mental health is a critical issue that affects millions of people worldwide. It can be caused by deep wounds such as depression, anxiety, and panic attacks that can take a toll on our physical and emotional well-being.

By understanding the root causes of these problems, we can start to overcome them and no longer allow them to create a battlefield in our minds. By releasing fear, we can create space for healing and growth. This requires an honest look at ourselves and being willing to face the darkness within us in order to move forward with courage and grace. With the right tools and resources, anyone can learn how to manage their mental health issues more effectively. When healing from wounds of the mind, we must understand it's a process. It's normal to experience many emotions.

Fear and pressure can both play a huge role in battling these issues. As we begin to heal from this wound, we must seek God and ask Him for specifics about the root cause of our anxiety, depression, or panic attacks. Being honest with ourselves on this journey is key.

For me, seeking God, going to the doctor, and acknowledging where I was emotionally, mentally, and physically helped start the healing process of this wound. I was also given some tips for managing panic attacks naturally, keeping me focused and at peace.

Tips:

- Slow deep breathing. Inhale through the nose (four seconds) and exhale through the mouth (six seconds). Do this for a total of three times or until you feel a calmness.

- Focus on something positive. This can be nature, family, scriptures, affirmations, etc.

- Count backward. I would sometimes start at 20, but feel free to start where you want.

- Remove yourself from toxic people and situations. I understand this tip isn't easy for everyone, but please try and start somewhere or contact a professional for help and resources.

- Diet Change. A lot of times, what we eat, or lack thereof, can alter our mood and mindset

- I am unsure what your healing process may look like, but I pray the tools I share will help you along your journey.

Let's heal and overcome

I learned that I can control my thoughts and no longer had to come to an agreement with every thought that came into my head.

I embraced having a choice.

Limit thinking on the past or future. Too much of both can be detrimental.

Write in a journal when you notice something or someone triggering you.

Exercising helped a lot, and I found myself feeling more peaceful than normal.

Focus on some scriptures about overcoming anxiety and allow them to be your focus for that day.

In most cases, a diet change can truly help out a lot. Sometimes the foods we eat contain substances which can cause us to experience physical reactions such as irritability or anxiety. I noticed this with myself, so I suggest checking out a book authored by Dr. Peter J. D'Adamo, called "Eat Right for Your Type." This book recommends things you should stray away from. Also, try to note how you feel when you eat certain foods. I find that caffeine, sugary foods/drinks, and alcohol can affect your overall physical and mental health.

Change the environment. Again, I understand that this isn't that simple for everyone, but for those that can, I truly believe this can help you be more at ease.

Talk to someone. Sometimes, we have to vent, and if that means having a trusted friend, Christian counselor, or therapist, then so be it. Just open your mouth and start the process of living free from anxieties and panic attacks.

Pray

Father, Your Word says to cast all worry and anxieties onto You, so today, I'm releasing them all to You. Father, I speak to those things and command all worry, stress, fear, anxiety, panic attacks, nervousness, and the like, to leave me and go to the pit of hell to be burnt forever in the name of Jesus. Father, I pray that the same mind in Christ Jesus is in me. I thank You for peace of mind, a sound mind, and for delivering me from the hands of the enemy. Father, I speak Psalm 91 over myself and my loved ones. I pray I am able to live in peace, joy, love, and freedom in the name of Jesus. Amen.

What's T.R.U?

Yes, it's T.R.U that you may have experienced panic attacks, depression, or anxiety.

What's Truth?

God's Word says: "Finally, brothers, whatever is true, whatever is noble, whatever is right, whatever is pure, whatever is lovely, whatever is admirable-if anything is excellent or praiseworthy—think about such things." (Philippians 4:8 NIV)

"Casting all your anxieties on him because he cares for you." (1 Peter 5:7)

"Can any one of you, by worrying, add a single hour to your life?" (Matthew 6:27 NIV)

20

Forgiveness

Forgiveness isn't always about doing something for a human relationship but rather about being obedient to what God has instructed us to do. – Lysa Terkeurst

HEALING FROM UNFORGIVENESS DOES not happen overnight. Just like anything else, it takes a willing heart and Jesus. Our Heavenly Father will also forgive us when we forgive others who sin against us.[27] To some, this statement is hogwash, especially if you've tried forgiveness once and it never worked out for you. One day, a wise woman told me, "Forgiveness is not just one and done but a daily thing in some cases."[28] Paul tells us we should die to our flesh daily,[29] including the racing thoughts that keep us in bondage.

Forgiveness is not a feeling. We may not always "feel" like forgiving others, yet we say we desire peace. Ashley Ormon, a forgiveness coach, wrote: "Forgiveness is knowing and remembering what happened, but choosing to move beyond it." We can't turn back and change our past nor dictate how others respond to us. However, we can control how we respond. Hebrews 8:12 says, "For I will be merciful toward their iniquities, and I will remember their sins no more." The "I will remember their sins no more" in this scripture refers to God, not me or you! It refers to GOD! When we break this down, the word remember, according to the Greek narrative, translates to "reward or punish" or "to be mindful."

While no more means just that, "henceforth, any longer/more." Simply put, our sins were forgiven on the cross through Jesus! What a peace that scripture brings to one's heart.

Forgiveness does not mean you have to be in a relationship with people. They never have to be part of your life again. Maybe God is not telling you to buy your abuser a house and car like Joyce. However, He could tell you to put in the work required to heal whatever unforgiveness looks like in your life. Below are some coping mechanisms many of us use instead of forgiveness:

- Deny your pain and hurt;

- Overly optimistic or hyper-spiritual;[4]

- Trying to convince yourself that things were not as terrible as they seemed;

- Imagining how things should be versus what they are/were;[5]

- The person is dead;[6]

- You are still hurting, not ready to forgive;[7]

- Fear of repeated offenses;[8]

- You feel forgiveness won't help anything;

- You feel forgiveness will give the other party false hope that you want to reestablish the relationship;[9]

- They never apologized or acknowledged what they did was wrong;[10]

- The pain you experienced altered your life, and yet no one has ever validated what you went through was wrong. Especially a parental figure or those close to you;[11]

- Not the right time.

I can guarantee I have thought about all of these statements. I'm not here to take any of that away from myself or you because they are all valid reasons. But if we are being honest, we are denying ourselves the opportunity to live healed and whole in Jesus. The Bible says, "Be angry and do not sin; do not let the sun go down on your anger, and give no opportunity to the devil."[38] As humans, we are prone to covering things up. We all have a certain place we run to where it is dark rather than risk what may come out in the light. We want freedom but resist doing what God says to do.[39]

My journey was and still is rough on many occasions. Not all offenses took me overnight to overcome. Some needed more time as I let the Lord repair my heart moment by moment. I felt forgiveness required restoration, and others had to own up to their stuff for it to be official. I thought those who wronged me had to suffer. I held grudges for years and thought I needed to physically see God paying them back for what they did or said to me. But I read a story that changed my perspective. Matthew 18:15-22 discusses what to do when our brother sins against us. Our instructions are to:

- Go and tell him his fault, keeping this between you two. If he listens, you've gained a brother.

- If he doesn't listen, take two or three others with you as witnesses. If he continues to ignore them, tell the church.

- If he refuses to listen to the church, let him be to you as a Gentile and a tax collector.

- We should forgive our brothers who sin against us seventy times seven.

The one thing that stuck in my heart from this passage was; a relationship with Jesus requires me to surrender any unforgiveness towards others. This is in order to experience true repentance, worship, and peace.

————◆———

Matthew 18:23-35 discusses the "Unforgiving Servant." In this parable, Jesus shares how the kingdom of heaven is compared to a king who wanted to settle accounts with his servants. Two servant men had debts to pay. As a result of his compassionate heart, the king released ten thousand dollars in debt to the first man. That same man, who was forgiven, ventured out and found servant two. This debt was much lower, more like one hundred dollars. Well, servant two pleaded for patience with servant one. But he did not extend the same grace given to him by the king. The first servant seized him, choked him, and put him in prison until his debt was paid. When their fellow servants saw what had taken place, they reported it to their master, the king. In return, the king called the first servant a wicked servant. In his anger, the king delivered the first servant to the jailers until his debt was paid in full. It was no longer possible for servant one to be forgiven of his debt without punishment or consequence.

This story had me in tears, especially when Jesus says at the end, "So, also, my heavenly Father will do to every one of you if you do not forgive your brother from your heart." Are you currently keeping someone indebted to you and yet seeking to have yours released?

————◆———

Let's heal and overcome

Healing unforgiveness requires us to acknowledge that something needs forgiveness. Each situation is different. Forgiveness is a choice, and we must choose to heal daily. What we hold onto in unforgiveness reveals deeper issues within ourselves and hinders our growth spiritually. Let's reflect and think briefly about the following:

- A time when you forgave someone, or they forgave you, and the relationship was restored.

- When you forgave someone, and no restoration was given.

As you reflect on your answers, have you noticed a distinction between the two questions? For me, my reflection was clear. The first question shows reconciliation. This requires both parties to work together. For many years I found it difficult to forgive and reconcile with the people I admired and had close connections with. Mainly because I was naive in believing those people were close to absolute perfection. On the other hand, it was easy for me to forgive toxic relationships because their poisonous nature was familiar and comforting to me. How toxic is this thinking? Yet, I know I'm not alone. The pain of healing a broken heart when it's bruised by someone with a deep connection may take years to repair. Being around them worsens it.

This leads me to our next healing point. God does not require you to physically be next to others to ask for or give forgiveness. All He needs is your heart to match your words. We can't force others to change nor demand an apology for what we know, feel, or think they did wrong. When understanding the adage "Hurting people hurt people," we can quickly identify why boundaries are needed for growth, protection, and healing. Forgiveness releases our need for retaliation, not our need for boundaries.[40] Compassion works hand in hand with forgiveness. Without it, you can become frustrated, lose your peace, and become bitter, angry, and rude. Without boundaries, their poor choices will bankrupt your spiritual capacity for continued compassion.[41] Not forgiving someone isn't teaching them a lesson or protecting you anyway. It's choosing to stay in pain and avoid dealing with pain; a mind at peace cannot coexist.[42]

Have you or someone you know ever pointed fingers and complained about how you or they feel they are the ones always having to forgive, apologize, reach out first, or do right while others get a free pass? My cousin once quoted me, "Instead of asking God why me," your words and heart should turn to "Why not me, God?" God wants to use each of us to advance His kingdom because our lives are not ours. My prayer for you is that as you ask yourself that same question, why not you?

Below, I will leave you with some questions to answer when facing a situation where forgiveness is needed. I was given these same questions, and my reflection helped me forgive. I pray they help you too.

1. What are their most realistic and unrealistic expectations of me? What is my most realistic and unrealistic expectation of them?[17]

2. What boundaries do I need to put in place?[18]

3. What must I do in this relationship to stay consistent in my character, conduct, and communication?[19]

4. Do I feel freedom in this relationship to communicate what I can and cannot handle without the fear of being punished or rejected?[20]

5. God, does this relationship need restoration or separation?

Pray

Father God, in the name of Jesus, I ask that You search my heart today. Please show me the things I need forgiveness for and the things I need to forgive others for. Your word says, "Forgive us our trespasses as we forgive those that trespass against us." Father, I pray for a heart of gentleness, humility, peace, compassion, love, faith, and trust in You. Father, I ask that I learn to forgive daily and stop pushing others away because of the hurt only a few people have caused. Father, forgive me for my sins, known (Name them _____) and unknown. Free me from the spirit of offense and help me grow in faith to see people the way You see them. Give me wisdom and discernment in knowing what a healthy relationship looks like. Please give me the strength and courage to let go of who needs to be released and to enjoy the ones I need to enjoy genuinely. Teach me to be slow to speak, quick to listen, and slow to become angry. Amen.

What's T.R.U.?

Unforgiveness was holding you back from your freedom. Some situations are too painful to let go of. You may not feel like forgiving.

What's Truth?

God's Word says: "If we confess our sins, He is faithful and just to forgive us our sins and to cleanse us from all unrighteousness." (1 John 1:9)

"Pay attention to yourselves! If your brother sins, rebuke him, and if he repents, forgive him, and if he sins against you seven times in the day, and turns to you seven times, saying, 'I repent,' you must forgive him." The apostles said to the Lord, "Increase our faith!" (Luke 17:3-5)

"For you, O Lord, are good and forgiving, abounding in steadfast love to all who call upon you." (Psalm 86:5)

21

Redefining Your Now

One of the reasons many of us have a difficult time dealing with our past is because we aren't able to differentiate between trash and recyclable material. - Evan and Jenny Owens

REDEFINING YOUR NOW IS when we choose to embrace healing and transformation. It is about taking an honest look at our past. It is about recognizing the wounds we carry from trauma, shame, and unforgiveness and finding the courage to face them. It is about finding peace in the present moment and creating a life that honors who we are now and who we want to become. Through this process, we can create a more fulfilling life by learning to forgive ourselves for our mistakes. We can also heal our past wounds and make conscious choices that bring joy into our lives.

Though this is only the beginning of the next chapter in your life, I want to encourage you to keep pushing forward. Your past wounds do not have to define your present. God wants to use your pain for a purpose. But it's important we remember to acknowledge our wounds. Secondly, we should fully commit to healing that wound, even if it hurts a little. As the Japanese writer Haruki Murakami once wrote: "Pain is inevitable. Suffering is optional."

Committed to healing

Healing from past traumas and wounds requires commitment and dedication. It can be a difficult journey, but it is also incredibly powerful. To fully commit to healing, we must be willing to take the necessary steps to make it happen. We must use our voices to help others who have lived through similar experiences and strive to create a more compassionate and understanding generation.

We can start by talking to God. It's in this intentional space where we can be honest and surrender all of our burdens. The following S.T.A.R steps can be done in no particular order:

- **S**etting small goals for ourselves

- **T**aking time for self-care

- **A**llowing ourselves the space to process our emotions in healthy ways.

- **R**eaching out for support when needed

Taking these steps will help us heal past wounds and embrace the future with hope.

Can I be honest with you? I have not always enjoyed my healing journey. It's much easier to embrace avoidance or approach every issue with warm hugs and smiles, acting as if nothing bothers us. Some may call it wearing a mask. However, healing can be arduous and ugly. After years of starting and stopping, I have found many tools and resources. I've spent countless hours wasting my time and gaining useful knowledge. Up until now, the most valuable knowledge came from reading my Bible, bumping my head, my support village, a child's movie, and two books. Combining all that together in just one book would've been overwhelming to read. Therefore, I've decided to share one of my favorite tools that's helped me stay committed to my healing.

This tool has been summarized in The Healing Equation.[47] Created by Evan and Jenny Owens, this equation helps wounded people break these patterns:

Denying;[48]

Crying;[49]

Numbing;[50]

and Running.[51]

Instead:

Acknowledging our wounds and taking personal responsibility for our healing.[52]

Grieving well. Forgiving ourselves and others while releasing shame and unforgiveness.[53]

Allowing ourselves to feel and heal the roots of our wounds.[54]

Establishing our identity in truth so we can face whatever lies ahead.[55]

It's presented in a simple manner, yet it is packed with useful, life-changing information. After reading their book, I realized I'd been on the right track all along. Still, their equation put into words my years of research and personal experiences. It helps us navigate our journey with a solid foundation.

The Healing Equation

Safety + Stability + Support = Healing

Safety is about reliability and trust. It's the essential ingredient for healing. God is our shelter and foundation, reliable and trustworthy. He alone can carry our wounds. Safety walls can also be found in individuals and communities. This is the sum of walls to lean on. Offering mental, emotional, and spiritual support to heal and heal well.[56]

Stability is a state of stillness and predictability that enables us to improve our lives.[57] It gives us normalcy and routine. This requires us to take into account that our wounds may not have been our fault. However, it is our job to take personal responsibility for accepting what we can change in our own lives. This reminds me of Jesus' role and how we gain stability by following Him.

While building a support structure, we must be mindful of who we allow to hold our safety net.[58] My personal belief is that the net held by Holy Spirit is the foundation of our support. This step offers correction, guidance, encouragement, and practical help when one truly needs help to get back on track. This is also a long-term need to help with resilience.

Jesus sent his disciples out in pairs. That is our reminder that we truly shouldn't do life alone, and I'm not talking only about marital relationships. Finding a trusted friend, mentor, Christian community, coach, therapist, pastor, etc., can do a lot in helping to keep you supported.

Knowing who you are

Once you have gotten through a lot of the steps mentioned throughout this book and can finally accept your identity in Christ, you can embrace your healing. You can genuinely believe you are a beloved child of God, deeply loved, forgiven, and accepted. In the same way, understanding you have a purpose, you have been chosen, and you are part of Christ's royal priesthood. With this in mind, you can start to see yourself the way God sees you and to accept the love, grace, and joy He offers you. From this place, you, too, can live out your God-given destiny and purpose. Using your voice to speak things that are not, as though they are.

———————◆———————

Let's continue the journey to heal and overcome

In the end, our ultimate goal is to move forward in our healing. I'm proud of you for making it this far in the book and look forward to possibly sharing your testimony on the website[59] or welcoming you into our women's group one day. As I thought of ways to summarize everything, I found the National Council for Mental Wellbeing did an amazing job. According to their website[60], we should do a check for the following, and if we have any of these symptoms, we should seek help right away:

- *Symptoms Of Trauma*

- *Headaches, backaches, stomachaches, etc.;*

- *Panic and anxiety;*

- *Changes in: sleep patterns, appetite, and interest in sex;*

- *Constipation or diarrhea;*

- *Easily startled by noises or unexpected touch;*

- *Weakened immune system;*

- *Fear, depression, PTSD;*

- *Nightmares and flashbacks, re-experiencing the trauma;*

- *Isolation, shame, survivor guilt, and self-blame.*

In turn, they also give helpful coping strategies to help manage the above symptoms:

- *Acknowledge you have been through a traumatic event;*

- *Connect with others;*

- *Exercise;*

- *Relax;*

- *Take up music, art, or other diversions;*

- *Maintain a balanced diet and sleep schedule;*

- *Avoid overusing stimulants such as caffeine, sugar, and nicotine;*

- *Commit to something meaningful or important daily;*

- *Write about your experience for yourself or share it with others.*

Healing can look different for each person. It generally involves finding wholeness and restoration in the mind, heart, and spirit. Breaking free from trauma can involve seeking professional help, processing your emotions, and developing healthy coping mechanisms. Forgiving others can be a difficult process, and it requires letting go of resentment and choosing to extend grace and mercy. It is important to remember that the healing process is a journey, and it takes time and effort. It is not a linear process, and it requires patience and self-compassion. Taking care of oneself mentally, physically, emotionally, and spiritually is essential for a successful healing journey.

Overall, the goal is to take back the power and authority your voice truly carries. You cannot allow your unhealed wounds to keep you in bondage and living in the past. Instead, you must "Redefine Your Now." This will require faith, forgiveness, courage, resilience, and strength - but it will be worth it in the end!

Pray

Father, I thank You for who You are. I thank You for Your son, Christ Jesus, and Your Holy Spirit. Father, I am thankful for Your unconditional love. Lord, I surrender all of my wounds to You (name the wounds_____) as well as those I no longer remember. Father, I ask You to forgive me for the role I played in my: shame, trauma, rejection, and unforgiveness. Father, I forgive (name those that you need to forgive, including yourself), and I surrender the weight of each person I've been carrying to You. Father, I thank You for giving me the strength, peace, and faith to heal well through such hurt and pain. I thank You for healing my broken heart and stitching up my wounds. I thank You for restoration, peace, joy, love, and for turning my pain into purpose. I thank You for keeping me another day in Your grace and mercy. I thank You for the freedom of choice and being able to choose You daily. To trust You and commit to my healing journey. In Jesus' name, I pray. Amen.

If you enjoyed this book, please feel free to leave a review on the website at https://www.warriorwomenic.com

Acknowledgements

I want to start by thanking my amazing husband, Brian. I appreciate the nights you cooked dinner and took the children out so that I could focus on writing. To our children, thank you for supporting Mommy as I endured long nights and many days trying to finish this book. Thank you all for fasting with me and loving me through the days I had to re-live moments. You all believed in me when I didn't believe in myself. Children: I pray this book is a tool to help you avoid falling into the pitfalls I fell into. Learn from Mommy and be better! Brian; you, Josh, and Helen believed that I could design my own book cover, and I appreciate you all for pushing me to use my gifts.

To all my friends, family, and prayer warriors, you all kept me focused and held me accountable. Apostle Henry, Delphine, Chelsea, Tisa, U. Robert, Sonia, Trece, Amber, Tae, Maisha, Wilma, Cortland, The Warrior Sisters on MP, and many, many, more.

To my father for being one of my biggest supporters and encouraging me through every chapter. Thank you for never judging me and for supporting me in sharing my truth. Thank you for being an example of what a restored relationship looks like. And for your many prayers.

To my beta readers: Nyenye Jordan, Pamela D. Smith, Keana Hughes, and Karen Stacy. Thank you for reading chapter two of my book. I know it went from a devotional to a memoir, but that's the beauty of beta readers. Your feedback helped in many ways. May God bless you each in all you do.

To Yuri Kenan, your patience with me was impeccable. I thank you for believing in me and holding my hand through this process. You were my doula, and when it was time to deliver, God made room for me to be handed over to my midwife Harriet D.C. T., and now we have a completed book. Love you, sis.

To everyone that has played a part in the birthing of this book, it's too many to name. Just know I love each and every one of you.

Further Reading And Resources

The following recommendations are not affiliated with the author or publisher of this book. In no way is the author or publisher of this book being compensated for this section.

Recommended Books

Bevere, John. The Awe of God: The Astounding Way A Healthy Fear Of God Transforms Your Life. Nashville, Tennessee: W Publishing, 2023.

De Salvo, Louise, Ph.D. Writing as a Way of Healing: How Telling Our Stories Transforms Our Lives. Boston, Massachusetts: Beacon Press, 2020.

Meyer, Joyce. Battlefield of the Mind: Winning the Battle in Your Mind. New York, New York: Warner Faith, 2011.

Owens, Evan and Jenny Owens. Healing What's Hidden: Practical Steps to Overcoming Trauma. Grand Rapids, Michigan: Revell, 2022.

Strongs, James, The Strongest Strong's Exhaustive Concordance of the Bible. Eds. John R. Kohlenberger III and James A. Swanson. Grand Rapids, MI: Zondervan, 2001.

Terkeurst, Lysa. Forgiving What You Can't Forget: Discover How To Move On, Make Peace With Painful Memories, And Create A Life That's Beautiful Again. Nashville, Tennessee: Nelson Books, 2020.

The Holy Bible (Whatever version you feel comfortable with)

Van Der Kolk,Bessel, M.D. The Body Keeps The Score: Brain, Mind, And Body In The Healing Of Trauma. New York, New York: Penguin Books, 2014.

Warren, Rick. The Purpose Driven Life: What On Earth Am I Here For? Grand Rapids, Michigan: Zondervan, 2012.

Film Recommendation

Konzelman, Chuck, and Cary Solomon. 2019. Unplanned. United States: Pure Flix Entertainment.

Recommended Resources

- American Association of Christian Counselors

Website: https://www.aacc.net/

Phone: 1.800.526.8673

- Crisis Counselor Text Line

For: Anxiety, Eating Disorders, Depression, Suicide, and Self-Harm

Text HOME to 741741 to connect with a volunteer Crisis Counselor 24/7

- (Emdria) EMDR International Association

Website: https://www.emdria.org/.

- Good Grief

For: All types of grief tools and resources for the entire family

Phone: 908-522-1999

Website: https://good-grief.org/resources/

- National Domestic Violence Hotline

Phone: 800.799.SAFE (1.800.799.7233) 24/7

Text START to 88788

Website: https://www.thehotline.org

- National Sexual Assault Hotline (RAINN)

Phone: 800.656.HOPE (1.800.656.4673) 24/7

Website: https://www.rainn.org

- We Rescue Kids (WRK)

Website: https://www.werescuekids.org

Phone: 1.531.541.5437

1. "How to Manage Trauma," National Council for Behavioral Health, accessed April 28, 2023, https://www.thenationalcounci l.org/wp-content/uploads/2022/08/Trauma-infographic.pdf

2. Merriam-Webster Online, s.v. "wound," https://merriam-webste r.com/dictionary/wound

3. Psalm 147:3 (ESV)

4. Jeremiah 30:17 (ESV)

5. The story of Cain's murder of Abel and its consequences is told in Genesis 4:1–18

6. 2 Samuel 13:1-22 records the rape story of Tamar, daughter of King David.

7. Housman, Patty. "Roe v Wade Overturned: What It Means, What's Next." American University Washington, DC, June 29, 2022, https://www.american.edu/cas/news/roe-v-wade-overturn ed-what-it-means-whats-next.cfm.

8. Tara C. Jatlaoui, MD; Maegan E. Boutot, MS; Michele G. Mandel; Maura K. Whiteman, PhD; Angeline Ti, MD; Emily Petersen, MD Karen Pazol, PhD. "Abortion Surveillance – Morbidity and Mortality Weekly Report (MMWR)." Centers for Disease Control and Prevention (CDC) Accessed November 23, 2022, https://w ww.cdc.gov/mmwr/volumes/67/ss/ss6713a1.htm

9. Psalm 23:1-6 (ESV)

10. 1 John 1:9 (ESV)

11. Matthew 4:10 (NLT)

12. A clip from one of Joyce Meyer's Testimonies' of forgiveness ht tps://www.youtube.com/watch?v=bqw7x5Twj64

13. Ramis, Harold. 1993. Groundhog Day. United States: Columbia Pictures.

14. See: https://www.urmc.rochester.edu/encyclopedia/content.aspx?contenttypeid=135&contentid=346
   "The University of Rochester Medical Center explains, "A ruptured cyst can cause more severe symptoms. These can include bleeding and severe pain in the lower belly. Symptoms like this need immediate treatment, which means the doctor may remove the cyst or your entire ovary.""

15. https://www.mayoclinic.com ,defines "colposcopy" (a procedure to closely examine your cervix, vagina, and vulva for signs of disease)

16. https://www.johnshopkins.com , defines "cervical biopsy" (a procedure to remove tissue from the cervix to test for abnormal or pre-cancerous conditions or cervical cancer)

17. Kubler-Ross, David, and Elisabeth Kessler. 2014. On Grief and Grieving. London, England: Simon & Schuster.

18. "How to Manage Trauma," National Council for Behavioral Health, accessed April 28, 2023, https://www.thenationalcouncil.org/wp-content/uploads/2022/08/Trauma-infographic.pdf

19. Mamoulian, Rouben.1931. Dr. Jekyll and Mr. Hyde. United States: Paramount Pictures.

20. Psalms 25:18 (NLT)

21. Romans 12:21 (NLT)

22. Genesis 9:20-23 (ESV) shares the story of Noah in his drunkenness state.

23. Genesis 19 (ESV) shares the story of Lot and his disturbing story of the issues that can present themselves from drunkenness.

24. Lawrenz, Lori, PsD. Commom and Unique Phobias Explained. Accessed June 5, 2022 https://www.healthline.com

25. Definition of reverential. https://www.vocabulary.com/dictionar y/reverential

26. The story of Moses and his feeling incompetent, Exodus 4

27. Matthew 6:14 (ESV)

28. B. Mack, personal communication, September 20, 2022.

29. Luke 9:23 (ESV)

30. Terkeurst, Lysa. Forgiving What You Can't Forget: Discover How To Move On, Make Peace With Painful Memories, And Create A Life That's Beautiful Again. (Nashville: Nelson Books, 2020), page 16.

31. Ibid p. 20

32. Ibid p. 17

33. Ibid p. 16

34. Ibid

35. Ibid p. 17

36. Ibid p. 16

37. Ibid

38. Ephesians 4:26-27 (ESV)

39. Terkeurst, Lysa. Forgiving What You Can't Forget: Discover How To Move On, Make Peace With Painful Memories, And Create A Life That's Beautiful Again. (Nashville: Nelson Books, 2020), page 8.

40. Ibid p. 127

41. Ibid p. 132

42. Ibid p. 202

43. Ibid p. 134

44. Ibid

45. Ibid p. 133

46. Ibid

47. Owens, Evan and Jenny Owens. Healing What's Hidden: Practical Steps to Overcoming Trauma. Ebook edition. Grand Rapids, Michigan: Revell, 2022. Page 205

48. Ibid

49. Ibid

50. Ibid

51. Ibid

52. Ibid

53. Ibid

54. Ibid

55. Ibid

56. Ibid

57. Ibid p. 212

58. Ibid p. 222

59. "Warrior Women in Christ" https://www.warriorwomenic.com

60. "How to Manage Trauma," National Council for Behavioral Health, accessed April 28, 2023, https://www.thenationalcounci l.org/wp-content/uploads/2022/08/Trauma-infographic.pdf htt ps://www.henationalcouncil.org

About the Author

Jessica Williams is a native Detroiter turned South Carolinian. She is the founder of the Warrior Women in Christ women's movement. She is an ordained minister, wife, mother, writer, podcaster, and entrepreneur. For many years she suffered due to unhealed past wounds from trauma, shame, rejection, and unforgiveness. Now that God has healed her, she has a passion for helping others heal from their past and reclaim their voices.

Let's Connect

Email: jessica@warriorwomenic.com

Website: https://www.warriorwomenic.com

Instagram/Facebook: @warriorwomenic

YouTube: Warrior Women in Christ

Made in the USA
Middletown, DE
18 July 2023

34840610R00094